Kals

THE DECLINE AND FALL
OF SCIENCE

THE DECLINE AND FALL OF SCIENCE

CELIA GREEN

HAMISH HAMILTON

LONDON

First published in Great Britain, 1976
by Hamish Hamilton Ltd
90 Great Russell Street London WC1

Copyright © 1976 by Institute of Psychophysical Research,
Oxford

SBN 241 89394 1

Printed in Great Britain by
Western Printing Services Ltd, Bristol

Contents

Acknowledgements

Acknowledgements are due to the following for permission to quote from copyright material in the books or journals indicated: Allen & Unwin Ltd.—Bertrand Russell, *A History of Western Philosophy* and *Human Knowledge, Its Scope and Limits*; Collins, and Routledge & Kegan Paul—C. G. Jung, *Memories, Dreams, Reflections*; Routledge & Kegan Paul—C. D. Broad, *Religion, Philosophy and Psychical Research*; Gerald Duckworth & Co. Ltd.—John Passmore, *A Hundred Years of Philosophy*; Allen Lane The Penguin Press—David Cooper, *Death of the Family*; Basil Blackwell and the Editor of *Mind*—G. E. Moore, 'Wittgenstein's Lectures in 1930–33'; Addison-Wesley Publishing Co., Reading, Massachusetts—Richard Feynman, Robert Leighton and Matthew Sands, *The Feynman Lectures on Physics*; John Wiley & Sons, Inc. —R. M. Eisberg, *Fundamentals of Modern Physics*; Oxford University Press—P. A. M. Dirac, *The Principles of Quantum Mechanics*; Princeton University Press—C. N. Yang, *Elementary Particles*; Cambridge University Press—Sir Arthur Eddington, *Space, Time and Gravitation*; The Editor, *The British Medical Journal*; the Editor, *Journal* and *Proceedings* of the *Society for Psychical Research* (hereafter abbreviated to 'S.P.R.') Detailed references will be found with each quotation.

Any case which is quoted in this book without a reference is drawn from material in the possession of the Institute of Psychophysical Research, Oxford. Proper names (christian names, surnames and place names) referred to in our subjects' statements have been replaced by pseudonyms or initial capital letters, which do not correspond to the true initial of the name, in cases where the real name might lead to recognition of the subject's identity.

I should like to acknowledge the unstinting assistance I have received from my colleagues at the Institute at all stages in the writing of this book, in particular Charles McCreery, William Leslie, and Christine Fulcher.

An Open Letter to Young People

To be a genius has never been too easy, granted the tendency of the human race to like frustrating them. It is no easier in this century than any other time. In fact, it is rather more difficult, as in this century it is believed that an unrecognised genius is impossible.

However, I have in Oxford a place in which it is possible to carry on the struggle for survival, and I am looking for people to join me. There are at present too few of us, and this makes the struggle for survival even more difficult.

I cannot give a brief summary of my ideas; they are original, and that means they are difficult to communicate. However, I have written a book, *The Human Evasion*, which while containing rather a small fraction of what I think, does give an introductory impression of my outlook. If you find this too uncongenial, I think you should not bother to get in touch with me to find out any more.

If, on the other hand, having read the book, you do want to know anything more about what I think, and to see whether you would like to join us, there is no alternative to coming to Oxford for a time.

Please write to me, in the first instance, care of the publishers of this book.

CELIA GREEN

Aphorisms

Only the impossible is worth attempting. In everything else one is sure to fail.

*

Research is a way of taking calculated risks to bring about incalculable consequences.

*

Astonishment is the only realistic emotion.

*

The fact that something is far-fetched is no reason why it should not be true; it cannot be as far-fetched as the fact that something exists.

*

It is axiomatic that the importance of a given thing cannot be determined by the number of people who are prepared to admit that it is important.

*

In the light of absolute uncertainty, possibilities are facts and emotions are actions.

*

The way to do research is to attack the facts at the point of greatest astonishment.

*

People accept their limitations so as to prevent themselves from wanting anything they might get.

*

The depth of human suffering is the measure of the aversion which the human mind has for reality.

*

It is inconceivable that anything should be existing. It is not inconceivable that a lot of people should also be existing who are not interested in the fact that they exist. But it is certainly very odd.

*

There is nothing so relaxing as responsibility; nor any relief from strain so great as that which comes of recognising one's own importance.

*

All the prisoners are so sensible. They wouldn't use a file in case they cut themselves.

*

No one says: The infinite is infinitely important; nothing in the world is more than finite, therefore it is easy to act uncompromisingly. The nearest they get to this is: Nothing is very important, so there is no point in being uncompromising.

*

The remarkable thing about the human mind is its range of limitations.

*

The object of modern science is to make all aspects of reality equally boring, so that no one will be tempted to think about them.

*

If you say to a theoretical physicist that something is inconceivable, he will reply: 'It only *appears* inconceivable because you are naively trying to conceive it. Stop thinking and all will be well.'

*

The human race has to be bad at psychology; if it were not, it would understand why it is bad at everything else.

*

When someone says his conclusions are objective, he means that they are based on prejudices which many other people share.

*

Philosophy should not teach you to be mistrustful of metaphysical questions, but of metaphysical answers. The unjustified assumptions which underlie the procedures of commonsense are at least as suspect as those which tell you how many angels can be placed on the point of a needle.

*

Philosophy thinks it has discovered that there are no absolutes. It has actually discovered that human beings have no way of being sure what is absolute.

*

What everyone has against Ludwig of Bavaria is not that he ruined Bavaria but that he supported a genius in the process.

*

The psychology of committees is a special case of the psychology of mobs.

*

If you stand up to the human race you lose something called their 'goodwill'; if you kowtow to them you gain . . . their permission to continue kowtowing.

*

The only important thing to realise about history is that it all took place in the last five minutes.

*

Society expresses its sympathy for the geniuses of the past to distract attention from the fact that it has no intention of being sympathetic to the geniuses of the present.

*

It is very easy to make someone into a failure; you have only to prevent them from being a success.

*

It is superfluous to be humble on one's own behalf; so many people are willing to do it for one.

*

If the human race would take death seriously there would be no more of it.

*

Equality: It is easier to make people appear equally stupid than to make them appear equally clever.

*

In the days of patronage by individuals you had to be dishonest to your patron; in the days of patronage by committees you have to be dishonest to everybody.

*

Democracy: everyone should have an equal opportunity to obstruct everybody else.

*

When people talk about 'the sanctity of the individual' they mean 'the sanctity of the statistical norm'.

*

The difference between an earned and unearned income—an unearned income might enable someone to do something; an earned income is a guarantee that he is wasting his time.

*

In an unenlightened society some people are forced to play degrading social roles; in an enlightened society, everyone is.

*

Only a hereditary aristocrat can be expected to recognise the confidence of genius; a plebeian or another genius would be too jealous.

*

Learned men who found favour with some prince could enjoy a high degree of luxury, provided they were adroit flatterers and did not mind being the butt of ignorant royal witticisms. But there was no such thing as security. A palace revolution might displace the sycophantic sage's patron; the Galatians might destroy the rich man's villa; one's city might be sacked as an incident in a dynastic war ... (Bertrand Russell, *A History of Western Philosophy*, p. 247.)

Learned men who could obtain a modicum of support from the few remaining capitalists could carry out intellectual activities in a modest way, provided they were adroit enough to form themselves into charities, and did not mind being exposed to the inquisitions of ignorant bureaucrats. But there was no such thing as security. Devaluation might halve the value of their money; the Labour Government might decide to do away with charities; their nation might decide to embark on another war ...

*

The socially-disapproved attitudes are attitudes which it is possible to get wrong; the socially-approved attitudes are attitudes which it is impossible to get right.

*

I wouldn't expect society to recognise ability, but it might leave a few loop-holes for it.

*

In an autocracy, one person has his way; in an aristocracy, a few people have their way; in a democracy, no one has his way.

*

You may despise fame; but if you do, you must despise the opinions of your neighbours.

*

Society is everybody's way of punishing one another because they daren't take it out on the universe.

*

'The Sabbath was made for man. And the universe too.'

*

'Social justice'—the expression of universal hatred.

*

'Society is for man and man for society.'

*

War is a very good way of lowering the standard of living so that everyone has to concentrate on keeping alive. If they do have thoughts about reality, they won't have time to write them down.

*

Society is a self-regulating mechanism for preventing the fulfilment of its members.

*

I cannot write long books; I leave that for those who have nothing to say.

CHAPTER 1

The Decline and Fall of Civilisation

THE recent peak of civilisation, centred on Western Europe, from which we are in the process of declining, was the highest that the world has known. At its height, it encompassed scientific and philosophical ideas which had not previously been formulated. However, in doing so, it brought about its own downfall. In both science and philosophy it came too close to areas of thought which the human race wishes to avoid. Consequently, it became necessary to plunge back into an intellectual dark age, and this is a process which the human race has already brought to quite an advanced stage in the present century.

Former civilisations of the world have shown that the human race has been less reluctant to develop cultures in which some degree of artistic or even literary attainment was possible than it has to develop cultures in which science and philosophy could flourish. No civilisation prior to the recent European one had much knowledge of science. It is remarkable how little scientific knowledge was possessed even by the Greek and Roman civilisations which were themselves the first outcrop of the European peak. Julius Caesar, for example, had no idea why the days varied in length as he went further north. And the Greeks, although they are supposed to have had notable philosophers, actually had no one who approached the insights of Hume or Berkeley. Nor, incidentally, has any other culture before the European possessed a philosophy which included an awareness of the uncertain status of the external world—unless, of course, you count the Indian doctrine of *maya* as a recognition that the external world may be hallucinatory. But a dogmatic assertion that life is illusory is a different matter from an analytical recognition that it may be, and this recognition is unique to the European culture at its recent peak.

At its recent peak, indeed, the European mind found itself in an uncomfortable position. In philosophy it had formulated the idea that the external world might be illusory, together with a number of other related and equally irrefutable ideas. In mathematics and physics the most obvious developments ahead of it were the evolution of ideas concerning higher dimensionality. In psychology, and indeed not only in psychology but also in physics, it was confronted by the phenomena which it chose to call 'psychical' or 'paranormal', such as telepathy and psychokinesis. Further to complicate its position, ideals of scientific objectivity had been expounded which made it difficult for these issues to be concealed.

In these circumstances, the European mind took refuge in a social and intellectual revolution. The social revolution was designed to make it impossible for individuals to think, or express inconvenient thoughts. It should be made impossible for anyone to have time to think unless he performed this function as a paid agent of society. Society, naturally, would know how to select in favour of those who thought in approved ways. While the social revolution has been fairly obvious, the intellectual revolution (or the abolition of dangerous thought) has attracted little attention. But the fact remains that in all operative fields of thought the human race has involved itself in positions from which, on their own terms, no advance is possible.

*

The human race does not naturally pursue knowledge. Science arose by accident in the brief space when one great orthodoxy was loosening its hold and the new great orthodoxy had not yet reached its full strength. The first orthodoxy was that of religion, which dominated the dark ages. The second orthodoxy is that of the belief in society, which is dominating the dark age now beginning.

*

The basic idea of communism is that it should be impossible for any individual, by any means whatever, to obtain for himself freedom to do what he considers worth doing, as opposed to living out whatever kind of life-cycle is decreed by the collective. This idea is certainly not a new one. It is exemplified by virtually all primitive societies, both past and present. This degree of repressive control of the individual is, almost invariably, associated with some form of communal ownership, since it inevitably follows that once the potentiality of individual ownership arises, so also does the possibility of individual liberation from the dictates of the collective.

Consider, for example, the Suebi, one of the tribes which lived in Germany in Caesar's time. It is to be presumed that, like other such tribes, they were not profoundly different in genetic composition from the modern Europeans who are descended from them at a remove of not so many generations. These Suebi held their land in common, and lived by the combined proceeds of herding their flocks and the systematic pillage of neighbouring tribes. They had a system by which half the population stayed at home each year to tend the communal flock, and half went away on pillaging trips. They wore animal skins, and were not well covered even by those. Their level of brutality was very high, and of culture practically nil. It was impossible for any individual born into this tribe to do anything with his life except act out the tribal pattern.

Unfortunately I find it only too plausible to believe that a majority of people today would ask nothing better than to return to a similar state. The question really is what induced the Suebi to adopt the notions of individual ownership, which they acquired from the Romans, sufficiently to become the ancestors of civilised Europe. It is to be supposed that this was because it gave some of them scope to acquire property and power over other people. The modern communist tells us that what motivates capitalism in the first place is the individual desire for profit and power over other people. I do not see why we should disbelieve the modern communist, who is no doubt engaged in projecting his own motives into the situation. He is a true descendant of the Suebi. No doubt the development of civilisation is always at first assisted by the fact that the first beneficiaries are not the intellectuals or the artistically gifted, but those who are best able to increase their possessions by such characteristics as brutality and treachery. The human race has no objection to characteristics like this, which it readily understands and sympathises with. Further, it is not people with characteristics like these who arouse its real jealousy.

Since self-interest is so commonly denigrated today, I should say that personally it does not upset me at all that the development of civilisation has probably always been based upon it, and not upon a disinterested desire for culture and the advancement of knowledge. I recognise that those features of the social situation which permit me to make my life at all tolerable are unintentional. None the less, I am glad they are there.

It has always been an accidental by-product of self-interest that it led to an abstract concept of individual possession, and hence of the right of the individual to decide certain things for himself, without reference to collective approval, within the limits of a rigidly defined and clearly-stated system of laws. Once this situation arose, it could not be prevented from offering opportunities for individual freedom to a class of persons whom it was never initially intended to benefit—artists and philosophers of various kinds who had motives quite different from those originally required to seize and defend property. Once there is an abstract idea of individual possession, and it is possible to transfer ownership by inheritance or gift, it is quite possible for there to be philosophers, poets and scientists, such as Schopenhauer, Shelley and Lord Cavendish, living on their private resources and doing work of which the human race as a whole would not appreciate the interest, in spite of the fact that their characters may not have been particularly distinguished in terms of a capacity for brutality, treachery, etc.

In fact, by the time that the notion of personal property has reached a certain degree of refinement and abstraction, it is no longer even true that the acquisition of a relatively large amount of it, which is to say of a large amount of personal freedom to decide things without reference to other people, requires the same characteristics of physical aggressiveness, etc., that were required in a more primitive stage of society, when it was necessary physically to repel invaders from any territory which one wished to hold. When the concept of personal property has become refined into an abstract form of capitalism, characteristics such as intellectual acumen and perspicacity are sufficient to amass a large fortune. In fact, with the advance of civilisation, the class of persons who possess a relatively large degree of freedom of choice, whether by acquisition or inheritance, comes to be approximately correlated with the class of persons possessing high I.Q.s.

It is, of course, when this point is reached, that a civilisation begins to crumble. An independent thinker such as Schopenhauer arouses people's jealousy in a way that Attila the Hun does not. People become morally indignant that it should be possible for anyone to spend his life doing what he thinks is worthwhile, without consulting other people. They remember that civilisation grew up in the first place out of people's desire for personal profit and power over other people, and they start to represent as an ideal that primitive state of society in which only one of these motives can be indulged. In the primitive, or communistic, state of society it is not possible to act effectively on the profit motive, but it is possible to gratify your desire for power over other people by observing them helplessly bound to the forms prescribed for them by tribal custom. Indeed, you may indulge your desire for power over other people's lives more directly than that if you become a witch doctor or a social worker.

*

What is unacceptable about capitalism is that it makes it possible for some people, sometimes, to have chances to do things that the collective does not want done. They may be things that the collective does not want done sufficiently to pay for, or they may be things to which the collective is actually opposed. In a capitalist society, that is one in which a person can own some freedom, it is possible to do as Schliemann did. He spent the first half of his life making a fortune, and in the second half of his life he used the fortune to go and dig up Troy.

Now it is difficult to do as Schliemann did, that is to say, to make your fortune in the same lifetime in which you intend to use it. It was only possible because he had a high I.Q. and lived in a society in which it was possible to apply this to making a fortune. Also, it is true that what he did with his fortune was something in which the majority of people have little or no interest. It follows that although what Schliemann did was difficult, it was not nearly difficult enough, and that is why we now have a capital gains tax.

There is a certain tendency for persons of high ability to have offspring of high ability. It follows that if Schliemann had taken too long making his fortune to be able to go and dig up Troy himself, he might have left his money to a descendant who might also have had a high I.Q. Even if this descendant had not wished to go and dig up Troy, he might have had some other ambitious idea of which the collective would not have approved. This is why Estate Duty is so important. It would be less necessary if ability were not inherited, but unfortunately, to a certain extent, it is.

CHAPTER 2

The Abolition of Facts

THE human race's favourite method for being in control of facts is to ignore them. One of the modern methods for doing this is to encourage everyone to believe that only a few extremely crude and simple facts need ever be taken into account, and that these should be related in a few stereotyped ways. Further, this process is to be applied on a massive scale, perhaps because the falsity of a facile generalisation about a million people on the other side of the world is less open to any possible contamination or complication by analytical thought than a facile generalisation about a single person who lives under the same roof as oneself (though it must be admitted that the human race is pretty efficient at not noticing the facts about that either).

So modern schoolchildren are encouraged to believe that they can and should solve the problems of the world with a few simple thoughts of the correct kind. Thus a teenager recently wrote to the newspaper that it must be wrong for meat to be sold in tins of dog-food when human beings were starving in Bangladesh.

Of course, this belief that any properly indoctrinated child can decide what everyone in the world ought to be doing better than they can decide for themselves, and without taking into account the side-effects and ramifying consequences of their simple prescriptions, is not really an entirely modern invention. Formerly, it was bound up with the belief in Christianity, and everyone who had learnt the rules knew that it was right to send missionaries to teach the native women to wear cotton dresses of suitable modesty and to recite pieces of Christian dogma. At the present time it has become fashionable to perceive that this process had side-effects which were of dubious benefit.

Nowadays it has become fashionable to teach a different kind of universal propaganda and to interfere with what people might choose to do for themselves in different ways.

This process has, of course, very direct applications to the doing of research. It is believed that anything worth doing can always be formulated into simple and readily comprehensible projects, justifiable by relation to one or two simple considerations and absolutely excluding all others. These projects are supposed to be totally quantifiable and predictable in advance, and explicable to any committee. This procedure is patently doomed as a method of doing research, since in order to find out anything which has never been known before, it is necessary to undertake some manoeuvres of which the outcome is uncertain. However, as a method for ensuring that no research of an upsetting kind can possibly be done, it is simply splendid.

In this connection, it might be pointed out that this Institute could certainly not have justified to anybody in advance the work it did on lucid dreams or out-of-the-body experiences. As the phenomena had not previously been recognised, it would have been practically impossible to do so. It would have been even more impossible for me to justify in advance spending time on the sequence of psychological analysis that resulted in my being able to do ESP. It was impossible to justify retrospectively, either. When we made a prediction about the outcome of an ESP experiment, crudely based on my psychological ideas, our academic acquaintances expressed surprise that the result was as predicted, but said it didn't count as a prediction, since they couldn't see why it was made.

*

It is fashionable to pour scorn on the social institutions and beliefs of the past as though human nature had recently undergone some radical change. But on examination it may be found to have remained very much as before.

For example, it used to be fairly obvious that people's chances in life did not bear too direct a relationship to their abilities and merits, but were subject to the law of chance, their economic circumstances, and the fairly universal indifference of other people to their well-being. However, people wanted to be able to feel that there was nothing they themselves need do about any manifest discrepancies in the situation, so they put forward the theory that the circumstances of everyone's life were divinely ordained, so that there was no need to think any further about it.

This theory is now the subject of particular scorn, but the psychological assumption that everyone's needs are precisely met by his position in society is actually more unquestionable than ever. At least, this assumption is made with great firmness in the only case that really matters, which is that of a person of high ability expressing frustration at not being able to do something of which he cannot convey the importance to other people. For example, a friend of mine told his mother that I was a genius, to which she replied, 'Oh, but that's impossible. If she were she would be recognised. Nowadays, there is universal education.' As a matter of fact, it seems to have escaped the modern attention that geniuses of the past were not distinguished by a capacity to function very comfortably in the educational situation, even before this became universal and dominated by the prevailing ideology.[1]

Of course, I know that this case is a very rare one. High ability is uncommon, the inclination to use it to any effect is more so, and the capacity for being frustrated in any significant way practically never occurs in human nature. I am, of course, aware that in all other cases the human race expresses great concern that everyone should express their abilities to the full, and never more so than when those abilities are non-existent.

It should be borne in mind that it is necessary to frustrate only a very few people in order to ensure the decline of civilisation.

*

Another reason someone once gave a friend of mine why I could not possibly be a genius was that I did not get a First Class degree. The supposition that social assessments of the individual are *all* that need be taken into account in passing judgement on him is, of course, an interesting application of the belief that all facts not recognised by society should be ignored.

It is actually rather remarkable that I got a Second Class degree, at the appallingly advanced age of twenty-one. I taught myself to read at about the age of eighteen months and always had the degree

[1] '. . . It may safely be said that a very small proportion of the men of genius who have visited our universities have presaged their after fame by high academic distinction.' (Professor Sully, quoted in Havelock Ellis, *A Study of British Genius*, Hurst & Blackett, London, 1904, p. 148.)

of precocity and inclination towards intellectual pursuits implied
by that fact. In early childhood and in adult life, my preference for
intellectual activity to any other form of entertainment has always
been total. I know that this is very wicked, but it is so.

I was never in any sympathy with the principles adopted by
those who had the control of my education. It was at all times
perfectly clear to me that my wishes, ambitions, temperament or
inclinations were the last things likely to be considered; but it
cannot be said that anybody got round to asking me what they were.
When I expressed them, they were of course rejected.

My academic and social ruin was made certain by the introduction of an age limit on the (then) School Certificate examination
when I was thirteen. I would, of course, have been capable of
taking it at a much younger age than 13, but no one had arranged
for me to do so, since that was not at all the sort of lines their minds
were working on. It is, of course, on social terms quite unthinkable
that being prevented from taking examinations with the speed and
in the profusion that one feels inclined could have the slightest
effect on one's life. Nevertheless, it did.

From then on my fate was sealed as certainly as that of a man
being prodded along a plank towards the waiting sharks. This I
knew, but no-one would listen to me, and I walked the plank to
the end.

It is curious that while one's education is the part of one's life
over the conditions of which one has least individual control, the
results of it are held to brand one irrevocably.

My education was not my affair, any more than a sojourn in a
prison-camp is something for which the prisoners are much
responsible. Personally I regard the outcome of it as an indictment
of those who did determine the terms of it, as is also the fact that
I have no nightmares but dreaming myself back in the time of my
education. Let the fact of my Second Class degree be blazoned as
publicly as possible and let it be set beside whatever I may achieve
in adult life.

Einstein was not noticeably successful at school and had a bitter
grievance against his University for not giving him a research
assistantship. But he had the dishonesty of his social conscience
(as indeed his work in physics also demonstrates) and he made
no fuss, even when he was in a position to do so, thus lending
tacit support to the fiction that social institutions are founts of

benevolence and objectivity, and that there is no need whatever to consider the potentialities of an individual of high ability as a separate concept from the extent to which society has permitted him any opportunity to make use of them.

I am not Einstein (as they were rather fond of telling me when I was at school) and in all the years of my suffering I swore to remember, and that in the day of my fame, if that day ever came, they should not secure my silence with belated social blandishments.

Yes, indeed. I got a Second Class degree. *J'accuse.*

*

The abolition of all facts which society does not care to recognise has been aided by the development of a psychological mythology, not too much of which is ever explicitly stated, but which has the effect of ensuring that a good many things cannot be said.

Cynicism, for example, is out of place in a socialistic society. Sayings such as 'a friend in need is a friend indeed' or 'put not your trust in princes, nor in the sons of men' are rarely heard in modern times. As soon as a person becomes an agent of the collective, he is above suspicion. 'Put not your trust in social workers' is unthinkable.

This is a curious development, if one thinks about it. The original premise seems to be that the human race has no natural tendency to do nice things for one another, so that if it has any inducement in the way of self-interest, it will immediately do nasty things to one another. In a situation dominated by the rule of the collective, in which no one can get anything nice to happen for themselves, and therefore there is no possibility of self-interest, the purest altruism will suddenly blossom forth.

This is not really the most logical conclusion from the original observations. That members of the human race have little inclination to do nice things for one another, especially if they suspect one another of any form of superiority, is hardly to be doubted. To this situation considerations of self-interest might provide a partial counterpoise. For example, the teachers of an exceptional child, if paid sufficiently richly by its parents to achieve actual results in teaching it, might overcome their natural desire to do it as much harm as possible. Of course, people are very self-sacrificing in this kind of way, and if they thought the child was really exceptional they might be prepared to forego a considerable amount of personal advantage rather than risk doing it any good. Still, they might have to give the matter a little thought before deciding.

The motive of self-interest, in fact, may well be considered to be the only one that ever restrained people in their desires to harm one another. If this is so, it is clear that in a Welfare State, where self-interest is eliminated, there will no longer be any check on people's desires to harm one another. Except, of course, that they will have to do it in ways compatible with the social conventions. Modern teachers, not paid directly by their parents but by the collective, have nothing to fear in doing their worst to any exceptional child that comes their way. Provided they do nothing the collective would take exception to. But this is a pretty easy requirement to meet. They are the ones who write secret reports on the child; the child doesn't write any reports on them, and even if it did, it would still be on a sticky wicket, as all the methods for damaging people psychologically are not recognised. They cannot possibly be recognised, as people want to be free to go on doing them.

*

The psychological mythology, it is true, has its positive aspects. In addition to implicit assumptions which have the invisible effect of precluding certain lines of argument, it contains a certain number of stereotyped myths concerning the ways in which psychology is supposed to work. To consider just one of these, there is a myth to the effect that if a child is 'pushed', that is, if it is allowed to live in an intense, intellectual and purposeful way at an age when such living can have a positive effect on its prospects in later life, it will spend the rest of its life sadly lamenting the 'normal' childhood which it might have had, full of activities such as kicking its heels, wondering why it was feeling so tired and hopeless, and generally doing nothing which might make other children, or their parents, or its teachers, feel jealous of it.

This myth exists because the reverse is true. What is true is that if the few people who might like living in an intense and purposeful way are prevented from doing so when they are young, they will find it very difficult to arrange the necessary circumstances for doing so when they are grown up, and will be forever haunted by unfulfilled desire.

CHAPTER 3

The Abolition of the Individual

THE abolition of the individual is related to the general abolition of facts. As Henry Ford observed, you could have any colour of car so long as it was black; and in the compassionate society your individual needs will be the object of deep consideration so long as they are identical with everyone else's—or at least, so long as they are identical with what everyone has agreed to recognise as their needs.

The notion of harm being done to individuals by collective control of his life is, of course, unacceptable. As has been already indicated, I do not regard my education as having been entirely felicitous, and I have had occasion to observe the reactions, both curious and stereotyped, which people produce on being told this. One of the most remarkable is to tell me, brightly and reassuringly, that I am still alive. The implication of this assertion is evidently that I have nothing to complain of so long as the human race has not actually killed me physically. The slate is supposed to be wiped clean. I am perfectly free to start afresh. On reflection, I have concluded that this reaction makes sense if it is supposed that it reflects the subconscious recognition that what the human race *really* wanted to do to me was to kill me dead. It stopped short of lining me up against a wall and shooting at me. The human race is aware of its magnanimity and thinks that I should appreciate it too.

I know a Professor who is said by his friends to be an archangel. What this means is that he is studiously polite and does not launch machinations to destroy his colleagues' careers. By reference to a base-line of physical murderousness, the human race feels that this qualifies him for archangelic status.

*

It is important to the abolition of the individual that no problems should ever have to be considered except on a collective basis. There may be collective bodies administering 'aid' or 'help' on predetermined and stereotyped terms to groups of this or that kind, but all needs falling outside the terms of reference of such groups do not exist. So when I have explained to people about my education I find that they are often very keen to extract from me some sort of agreement that things are all right now. Now there are schools for clever children, associations for the gifted child and what not. That has to make it all right. Nothing can ever slip out of joint again—can it? It is just my bad luck that I was born a bit too soon, before collective understanding of the needs of my particular group had been so splendidly developed. Of course, as an adult frustrated genius, I have plainly had it. There is no group scheme for administering aid to this section of the population. However, statistically, what does it matter? Other children are being born with high I.Q.s, and they are being given the right kind of collective understanding.

On the contrary, of course, I consider it my good fortune that I was born early enough to gain some advantage, fragmentary though it was, from the lingering remnants of individualism that lurked in some corners of the educational system. They must be even rarer by now.

Then, again, I am sometimes expected to endorse the supposition that the thing to do to help children with high I.Q.s is to give money to some organisation or association that exists 'for' them. As a matter of fact, I have the deepest suspicion of benevolence mediated by the collective. *Timeo Danaos et dona ferentes.* If anyone does wish to devote some money to the assistance of the high I.Q.s, I would suggest providing private incomes, inflation-proofed, for any children who can demonstrate sufficiently high ability sufficiently early in life. If they are any good, they will soon reach an age at which they find themselves unable to explain to anybody why they want to do what they do want to do. Some of them, in spite of their high ability, will no doubt do nothing. However, the cost of continuing to support them would be trivial compared with the cost of supporting all the unmarried mothers who are surreptitiously supporting unmarried husbands on the income which they receive from the state.

I suggest that the demonstration of ability very early in life be

taken as the criterion, because the human race is so good at preventing the expression of ability once the educational process has
begun. Of course, it is true that there may be some children of very
high ability who do not, for some reason, show their ability very
early in life. These could be, to some extent, provided for by the
provision of handsome financial rewards for exceptional achievement at any stage of the educational process, and also by impress-
ing upon all recipients of high ability incomes that, if they did not
have too much use for their income themselves, they should feel
it incumbent upon them to use their intelligence to discern the
presence in the landscape of exceptional individuals endeavouring
to do things of which they could not explain the importance to
other people, and to render them such assistance as they could.

*

There is no need for the individual to know his own mind, since
he is not entitled to the possession of any problems on which his
own opinion would be better than that of a trained social worker or
some other authorised adviser. Naturally, therefore, there is no
recognition of the conditions which may make the knowing of
one's own mind possible.

Cavendish used to communicate with his servants by means of
notes, and forbade them to speak to him. It is perhaps worth reminding people of the conditions which people such as Cavendish
arranged to facilitate their intellectual activities.

The modern academic world has, of course, progressively lost
any standards it once possessed for recognising intellectual activity
as such. This was inevitable once the intellectual life of western
civilisation was no longer primarily the affair of economically
independent individuals, or at least provided with its standards by
the presence of a sufficient number of such people. The modern
intellectual or scientist is supposed to function as a dependent
employee of the collective, and the modern academic is *par
excellence* the person whose life has consisted of successfully doing
what pleased other people. This situation could not but lead to
an abandonment of intellectual standards, and their replacement in
every field of thought by stereotyped rules for guaranteeing conformity. From time to time statistics are produced which demonstrate that more scientists are alive at the present time than in the
whole previous history of the human race. If the progress of

science were really dependent on such persons, it would be difficult to account for the difference between the rate of development of physics and psychology in the last century and in the present one.

Since criticism of the socially trained and recognised expert is not much practised these days, it may be interesting to recall some remarks of Schopenhauer (whose own work was made possible by the possession of a private income).

> So it is in the republic of letters . . . The only thing in which all agree is in trying to keep down a really eminent man, if he should chance to show himself, as one who would be a common peril. From this it is easy to see how it fares with knowledge as a whole.
>
> Between professors and independent men of learning there has always been from of old a certain antagonism, which may perhaps be likened to that existing between dogs and wolves. In virtue of their position, professors enjoy great facilities for becoming known to their contemporaries. Contrarily, independent men of learning enjoy, by their position, great facilities for becoming known to posterity; to which it is necessary that, amongst other and much rarer gifts, a man should have a certain leisure and freedom. As mankind takes a long time in finding out on whom to bestow its attention, they may both work together side by side.
>
> He who holds a professorship may be said to receive his food in the stall; and this is the best way with ruminant animals. But he who finds his food for himself at the hands of Nature is better off in the open field. (Arthur Schopenhauer, *The Pessimist's Handbook*, University of Nebraska Press, 1964, p. 474.)

It may be noticed in passing that, along with the abolition of the economically independent individual has gone a deterioration in the position of the potentially intellectual woman. It may be thought that the loss to science and to the intellectual world generally is not very great, as women have scarcely been notable contributors over the centuries.

However, it may be noted that at that apex of civilisation marked by serious research into psychical phenomena at the end of the last century, a number of academic ladies such as Mrs. Sidgwick, Mrs. Verrall and Alice Johnson were among those concerned. Their participation, like those of the men, depended upon the economic circumstances of their day, which included a plentiful supply of domestic servants.

When the supply of domestic servants began to fail, the first sufferers were the female members of the middle classes. Even today, in an upper-middle-class household, it may often be found that the position of the head of the family is not too drastically different from what it would have been a century ago, whereas his wife (who perhaps a century ago might have been writing novels or spending her time on psychical research) is now a full-time cook/housekeeper.

It cannot be said that the movement known as Women's Lib shows any real recognition of the conditions actually necessary for any sort of genuinely intellectual activity. What appears to be at issue is that it is recognised that the position of men has not, in the changing social situation, deteriorated as radically as that of women, and the solution envisaged appears to be to see that it does.

In fact, in the process, the women concerned appear determined to demonstrate as thoroughly as possible their identification with precisely those psychological attitudes which have always prevented women from achieving anything much, and make it least desirable that they should become any more liberated than they are. Basically, the psychological attitudes in question depend on a belief in society, and of the desirability of regulating individual freedom by collective prescription, even more ruthless and total than that which is found in the generality of men. It is, as far as I can gather, proposed that women should be liberated (as it is called) by social prescription and by regulations even more precise and restrictive than heretofore about what ought to be done and thought. The fact that a psychological outlook primarily devoted to belief in society is not actually the best for achieving anything can, as in other areas where it might prove an embarrassment, be dealt with by the normal modern procedure of changing the rules about what constitutes achievement. Modern physicists and philosophers actually believe in society far too hard to think straight; the rules have simply been changed so that now not thinking is regarded as the best possible way of doing physics and philosophy. I am sure that by similar methods it will be quite possible to divert attention from the fact that the female sex is in the habit of rendering itself completely non-functional for doing anything of any significance.

*

The human race is allegedly in favour of people making use of their abilities, and doing difficult things is supposed to be virtuous. However, it is necessary to distinguish between things which are intrinsically difficult and things which are difficult only because the human race is opposed to them.

The human race arranged for Pasteur to crawl through a little tunnel behind the boiler to do his experiments, and for Madame Curie to do hers in a cold and leaking shed. These two socially acceptable characters did not complain.

Doing something which is actually intellectually difficult and requires the full use of your faculties is not socially approved of. Consequently, to the extent that it is allowed at all, care is taken to see that only people who are well-adjusted socially will have any chance to do it. These people, it is hoped, will be immune to deriving too much benefit from it.

As a matter of fact, the human race is always *au fond* opposed to anyone doing anything which is actually intellectually difficult and requires the full use of their abilities. This is because it has beneficial effects on the health. Needless to say, this fact is not advertised, and as we all know, 'working too hard' is the most socially acceptable cause of ill-health and the monstrous evil from which school children need to be most carefully protected.

'Working hard' in the sense of spending a great deal of time struggling through tunnels behind boilers is a different matter altogether. Doing things which actually do not involve the use of more than a tenth of one's natural abilities, and doing them ten times slower than the natural rate, is not good for the health. In fact, it is totally exhausting.

Also, curiously enough, it gives rise to no sense of achievement whatever. If, on the other hand, one is ever able to get into a position in which one actually is using one's abilities to the limit, a sense of achievement does result.

This is in spite of the fact that wading through hindrances even to spend a small amount of time doing the tenth best thing in an uncongenial way is of course far more arduous, and requires far more effort (in a certain sense) than actually doing anything without the hindrances. At the same time, of course, in doing anything to which one's abilities are actually suited, one will function at a far higher energy level than one is likely to in struggling with unnecessary obstacles.

If anyone tried to get into a position in which they may be able to use their abilities, the human race will carefully arrange a good deal of boiler-tunnel crawling for them, and there is not the slightest guarantee that this will ever be allowed to lead to the merest commencement of doing anything interesting. In fact, if the human race has its way, it certainly will not.

The striking absence of discussion of this issue is, in itself, evidence that profound psychological tendencies are at work in this area.

*

Another area in which some kind of repressive force is clearly at work is that concerning money. Money is what makes individuals independent of society; it has always been regarded as idealistic to decry it. It is difficult to state the case for this rejection of money in analytical terms. At any rate, I cannot recall having seen it stated in such a way. On the other hand, a very good analytical case could be made out for the desirability of money, on the most idealistic of grounds—but never is.

The charms of money are distinctly under-represented in literature. There are no songs or poems extolling its virtues. This seems on the face of it strange. The claims of money to be celebrated in verse might well seem to be no less than those of faithful dogs, beautiful women, or jugs of wine. Consider, for example, the following sample of what might have been written (I make no attempt at metre; you may imagine it as a translation of Old English or Chinese):

> Money which soothes my woes
> Faithful and neverfailing support when all else turns against me
> Constant and reliable when men betray and deride me
> Ever-attentive to my smallest wish
> Providing me with a fortress of refuge much better furnished than my enemies would wish me to have
> Respecting all my needs which I could not possibly explain to a social worker or my GP. . . .

*

Money not only gives you freedom to do as you wish, it also gives you something to oppose to other people's wish to do nothing whatever for you. That is to say, if you are able to pay a sufficiently high salary, you can pay a tutor for your son. If he wishes to go on receiving this salary, and particularly if you pay him by results, he will have a motive of self-interest to oppose to his natural desire to see your son learning as little as possible. Similarly, if you have sufficient money to pay for a cook, you can pay someone to overcome their natural desire to leave you to cook for yourself. This desire will be particularly strong if they suspect that you are at all likely to be devoting yourself in any serious way to developing a new mathematical theory of the universe or writing symphonies.

Of course, this statement of the situation is already somewhat out-of-date. People are extremely resentful of being placed in this sort of situation, in which they can actually further their own interests by acting against their desire to frustrate other people, and so modern society has developed a system of safeguards designed to reduce such pressures to a minimum. For example, the unemployed are supported by the State. It follows that no one is actually forced to accept a high salary to act as someone's cook or tutor in order to avoid starvation. They will, most of the time, willingly accept a lower rate of pay in order to do something that gives them greater *job satisfaction*. Job satisfaction consists of knowing that you are not actually doing anything to increase any one else's freedom.

This is an example of the self-sacrifice of the human race. It is quite erroneous to suppose that self-sacrifice is something that is usually done to promote the interests of others. It is much more usually accepted as necessary to hinder them.

The fact that the traditions of the human race give no hint of this situation is not to be wondered at. The traditions of the human race are not designed to put anyone wise to the situation.

This kind of self-sacrifice is also shown in the tolerance which the human race shows of primitive conditions, the alternative being a level of civilisation in which it would be more difficult to ensure that all individuals were equally unfree.

Darwin describes two primitive races. One had a hereditary monarchy and had made many advances in the control of its environment; the other was extremely democratic and had not done so. I think we may fairly suppose that the latter group had known quite well what they were doing and were being deliberately self-sacrificing in the interests of egalitarian principles.

*

Let us suppose that there is something you want to do (e.g. scientific research). There are two ways of setting about it. You can either provide yourself with the money to do whatever it is, or you can try to persuade some person or persons who have the necessary money that they should support you in what you want to do. This is only a restatement of the old-fashioned statement that 'He who pays the piper calls the tune'. Someone has got to pay the piper; either you pay, and call it, or you try to persuade someone else that it is a good tune and they should pay for it.

It is nowadays regarded as morally desirable that only the collective should have any money with which to call tunes. You should not be able to do things by financing them yourself. The first thing you are likely to need is a private income and this, in itself, is wicked. You should not be able to do things by obtaining the patronage of one or two rich individuals, because there should not be any individuals rich enough to patronise you. You should not be able to obtain the money to do what you want from any group smaller than the agents of the collective-at-large.

This, of course, makes it virtually impossible to obtain the money to do anything, because it is the first principle of the collective-at-large that nothing may be done.

Now it is very difficult to convince a single rich individual that something clever and original should be done, but there is a small chance of finding a rich individual that you may be able to convince. The chance of convincing a committee, or a group of persons who either are, or conceive themselves to be, acting as agents of the collective, that something clever and original should be done is of course incalculably smaller, to the point of non-existence. This is of course exactly as it is intended to be.

Let us suppose that you have a one-in-ten chance of convincing a given rich individual that he would like to support you in what you are trying to do. Then, if the condition for support is that you should convince both members of a group of two rich individuals, your chances are reduced to one in a hundred. If you have to convince all members of a group of three, your chances are reduced to one in a thousand.

*

People are more willing to give money to groups than individuals. This is because people are incapable of cooperating, and everyone relies on the probability that the persons concerned would only be able to remain in a group if their primary motive was obstructionist, rather than progressive. So they are supporting the likelihood of nothing progressive getting done.

This is another form of the belief in committees rather than individuals. Individuals are supposed to be very liable to *misuse* funds. They are also, of course, more likely to use them—but this, in the normal world-view, would really count as a form of misuse.

CHAPTER 4

The Apex of Civilisation

THE human race has never been too keen on knowing much, in any clear-cut way, about its own psychology. This is probably not unrelated to the fact that the concept of the individual as independent of the collective has never been popular. If society is to pass judgement on individuals, or alternatively to understand them better than they understand themselves, it is desirable that the individual should not be regarded as too complicated a bag of tricks. Indeed, in the present decline of civilisation, the tendency is for the psychological factors which may be admitted to consideration to be more and more rigorously restricted to a few exceedingly crude and stereotyped considerations which, it is alleged, are fundamental to everybody without exception. Further to increase the impression that human psychology contains no lurking potentialities for surprise, the few psychological considerations which are left in the picture are supposed to be physiologically determined.

In order to feel really secure about the individual human being, it is desirable to believe that he has no consciousness. In this modern psychology receives subterranean support from modern philosophy which, as we shall see later, has been working for some time on the idea that there is no such thing as consciousness. The idea that somebody or something has no consciousness evidently makes human beings feel that they are freer to do whatever they like with it, as is shown by the story about Descartes unkindly throwing a cat out of the window to celebrate his belief that animals had no consciousness. This story is probably apocryphal, but its existence demonstrates the association of ideas in human psychology.

So it may be seen that the attempt to think in an objective, analytical and introspective manner about the facts of human psychology was a striking development. The beginnings of psychology, psychoanalysis and psychical research were located together at the apex of civilisation at the end of the last century.

The Society for Psychical Research was founded in 1882, by a group of Cambridge scholars. The most striking individuality among the founder members was Frederick Myers (1842–1901) who has never, it seems to me, received the recognition due to him as the effective founder of psychical research, even from those who have made a study of the development of the subject. Myers was somehow not the sort of person that people are easily inclined to give credit to. Undoubtedly he had a very high I.Q. He had been a precocious child, and his collaborator Gurney wrote of him, 'While I am reading a book, Myers is mastering a literature.' Furthermore, Myers was emotional. He was a minor poet, and he had a taste for the dramatic. Altogether, he was more obviously a genius than people find agreeable, and there is a tendency to feel that it would have been nicer if it had not been Myers who provided the initiative and driving force of the early Society for Psychical Research. There were so many other people concerned whose lives were more obviously devoted to the support and maintenance of the social structure, such as Professor Henry Sidgwick, Sir William Barrett, and so on. However, as a matter of fact Myers did provide the driving force of psychical research, and its rate of progress was never the same after his death, although a good many people continued to spend a very great deal of time on it.

Myers's work on the subconscious anticipated that of Freud. Myers, however, did not become famous because his observations on the nature and methods of operation of the subconscious mind, being less restricted in scope than those of Freud, did not have the same appeal. If everything in psychology is related to infantile sexuality, you may well manage to emerge with a feeling that the human individual is more, and not less, stereotyped and predictable than you thought before you had heard of infantile sexuality. If the subconscious is understood, as Myers understood it, to include the latent potentialities of inspiration, telepathy and psychokinesis, it is difficult to have quite the same comfortable feeling that your calculations can never be called upon to include the incalculable.

Those psychologists, such as Myers, who took such factors into account, did not become famous. Those, such as Freud, Jung and Adler, who restricted their scope sufficiently to contribute to everyone's feelings of having everybody else taped, did. Nevertheless, it must be admitted that even Freud, Jung and Adler were characteristic products of a higher level of civilisation than prevails at present. No new systems of psychology, demonstrating even so much original and analytical thought, are being originated at the present time. The findings of the originators have been painlessly absorbed in the form of simple and helpful dogmas. No original work of an introspective kind is being done in psychology. In Oxford, even the work of Freud, Jung and Adler is considered too daringly introspective and interesting to be permitted to form part of the syllabus for a degree in psychology. The only questions about psychoanalysis which are likely to appear on Oxford degree examination papers are of the type: Is it possible to justify the study of psychoanalysis?

Psychology and psychoanalysis struggled for, and gained, social recognition. This was perhaps because it was already foreseen that they could be integrated quite usefully into the decline of civilisation. Nowadays, the implicit assumption that everything is known about psychology by those persons suitably recognised by the state as knowing about it, forms a part of society's claim to unquestioned authority over the individual. It is interesting to note how the role of the psychiatrist, in fiction and in fact, has changed over the last thirty years. Once he was a suspect, romantic and outsider-ish figure, siding with the individual against society and pleading (usually in vain) in court-rooms for a profounder understanding of mysterious psychological forces. Today he is legion. His word is accepted without question in every court; he is the authorised agent of society and no individual can claim that there is more to his case than society has considered once a duly qualified psychiatrist has had his say.

Psychical research never quite lent itself to enlistment as an aid to the decline of civilisation, in spite of some brave attempts which have been made in certain quarters to represent the facts of telepathy as demonstrating that no man is an island, we are all members one of another, etc. For this reason, the development of psychical research, from its beginnings in 1882, was always almost clandestine, although for some time it received the attentions, with the expenditure of very considerable amounts of time, energy and even money, of a large number of persons of the highest social and academic standing. The social revolution did its work of ensuring that such people should have other things to occupy them besides doing research that nobody wanted done, and the volume of time and effort expended on psychical research petered out, although it continued to be a matter of interest (albeit usually rather passive interest) to a number of leading intellectuals until the present day.

CHAPTER 5

The Abolition of Thought

THINKING has always been regarded as a dangerous, and potentially anti-social, activity. The economically independent individual is in the process of being abolished, so the risk of his thinking can be (it is hoped) ruled out. But it is desirable, at least at the present stage in the decline of civilisation, that there should continue to be recognised forms of social activity which go by the names of physics, philosophy and so forth, and carried on by persons duly authorised by society to do so. This has required the elimination of any standards for recognising genuine thinking, and their replacement by socially agreed rules for the carrying on of seemingly intellectual activities.

This is, after all, only what was to be expected, bearing in mind that the desired objective was that thinking should cease to be an individualistic matter and should become a social activity, carried on only in accordance with rules which would preclude any untoward developments.

When there was some kind of a concept of intellectual activity *per se*, it was of course clearly the case that a person who could recognise a clear and convincing train of thought in one field could also do so in another. Nowadays, as we know, there is a standing dogma to the effect that it takes all of one person's time to keep up with one tiny specialised area in a given field of research, and that it is totally and absolutely impossible to explain the basic ideas of any branch of science or philosophy to anyone who is not a socially accredited expert in it. It is supposed that this state of affairs reflects the high degree of advancement of intellectual activity in this century, but actually what it reflects is the fact that dangerous areas of thought such as physics and philosophy have, at the present time, as near as possible no basic ideas to explain.

To learn to pretend that they have, in accordance with the social rules, may well be a rather time-consuming process requiring numerous years of training and experience.

*

To understand modern thought it is important to realise that the principal object of philosophy is to eliminate philosophy, of theology to eliminate theology, of physics to eliminate physics, and so on.

Let us consider the case of philosophy which, being most nearly concerned with basic problems of conceptual thinking, exhibits the development of the modern syndrome in a particularly typical and illuminating way.

The desire of Wittgenstein (the sacred figure of modern philosophy) to be rid of philosophy was scarcely a secret. Allowing for the obscurity with which he habitually expressed himself, in an endeavour to prevent himself from noticing that he was actually thinking, Wittgenstein made it as clear as he very well could that the object of the exercise was to develop what he called 'the language game' to a point at which philosophy could stop.

Incidentally, à propos the obscurity of Wittgenstein, I may say that I do not take obscurity in itself as any indication of profundity. It is a part of the modern social rules that obscurity is to be regarded in this way when it conduces to the correct emotional attitude. This is, in part, why it takes so long to learn to become a philosopher or physicist these days. Sentences such as some of those produced by Wittgenstein, for example 'The proposition is articulate',[1] would, in other contexts, elicit the most bitter scorn as being a meaningless use of language. However, one realises as a result of a sufficiently intuitive attention to the matter, that Wittgenstein's underlying intentions are excellent. He is aiming at the establishment of common sense, and the elimination of all unpleasant questions concerning one's own consciousness and the curious fact that one is existing. Consequently, his incomprehensibility is to be regarded as brilliant and admirable.

*

[1] *Tractatus Logico-Philosophicus*, Routledge & Kegan Paul, London, 1922, p. 47.

Modern philosophy shares with modern physics the belief that it has finally solved everything of any importance, and that nothing remains to be done but to tidy up a few loose ends in terms of the existing theory. (This, of course, will have to be done by experts who have learnt to pretend that there is an existing theory.) For example, a friend of mine was once having tutorials on linguistic philosophy at Oxford. She raised as a certain difficulty the question of how had human language ever evolved to include more sophisticated linguistic structures, and to incorporate new concepts as scientific knowledge advanced. This may not seem much of a problem to anyone but a linguistic philosopher, but since it is essential that thinking should be reduced back to verbal statement, and this back to the concrete and everyday situations in which the use of these statements was first learnt, it actually is a problem for a modern philosopher and was very gravely accepted as such by my friend's tutor. However, although she could not produce a solution just at the moment, she was confident that one would be forthcoming, as a result of a few more years' research work on the problem by the right kind of people. As a matter of fact, I can think of a solution myself, although I do not know whether it would appeal to her. The human linguistic and conceptual system was able to expand because primitive men were not trained in linguistic philosophy.

*

Since old-fashioned philosophy has been to so large an extent forgotten, perhaps I may summarise its principal findings, which were all related to what we may call the principle of total uncertainty. It is impossible to be sure that what we are looking at is really there, impossible to be sure that our apparent memory of even the most recent event is not a delusion, impossible to be certain that the object we leave in a room is identically the same when we return and not merely a precise reproduction of the one we left, and impossible to be sure that anything is ever causally related to anything else, no matter how many times they are perceived in close conjunction.

This principle of uncertainty gave rise to a famous philosophical dilemma, known as the Problem of Knowledge. The problem in question was to distinguish some kind of knowledge or of mental activity to which the principle of uncertainty did not apply. A considerable amount of thought was expended over a long period on attempts, frequently convoluted and never entirely conclusive, to delineate such an area of knowledge. This might have led people to suspect that there was in fact no such area, but modern philosophers have decided in their characteristic way that there is in fact no such problem. They demonstrate this by saying that what they see they know. A chair is standing in front of them in the room, they mean what they think they mean and will brook no argument.

An even more suspect version of this argument is to say that when they use the word 'know' in sentences such as 'I know there is a chair in front of me', they are using the word in the way in which it is customarily used in situations of this kind, and no further questions need or may be asked. The latter version is, of course, preferable, since it avoids reference to the awkward concept of 'seeing'. Modern philosophers base their arguments as little as possible on references to anyone's mental processes, because they realise that to do so plunges them straight into the realm of uncertainty.

*

Before modern philosophy realised that its task was to eliminate itself, philosophers were having a tendency to produce analytical discussions of the human situation. These discussions were frequently in part dishonest or evasive, but they were expressed with an unfortunate clarity which made the irrefutable portions of them clearly irrefutable.

Consider for example the following passage from Hume, in which he refers to the fact that, however thorough our scientific knowledge of the laws of nature, we can never be certain that they will continue to apply from one moment to the next, and that the future will be in any way like the past:

> For all inferences from experience suppose, as their foundation, that the future will resemble the past, and that similar powers will be conjoined with similar sensible qualities. If there be any suspicion that the course of nature may change, and that the past may be no rule for the future, all experience becomes useless, and can give rise to no inference or conclusion. It is impossible, therefore, that any arguments from experience can prove this resemblance of the past to the future; since all these arguments are founded on the supposition of that resemblance. Let the course of things be allowed hitherto

ever so regular; that alone, without some new argument or inference, proves not that, for the future, it will continue so. In vain do you pretend to have learned the nature of bodies from your past experience. Their secret nature, and consequently all their effects and influence, may change, without any change in their sensible qualities. This happens sometimes, and with regard to some objects: Why may it not happen always, and with regard to all objects? What logic, what process of argument secures you against this supposition?[1]

Even so recent a philosopher as Bertrand Russell was capable of pointing out: 'I might have come into existence a few moments ago, complete with just those recollections which I then had. If the whole world came into existence then, just as it then was, there will never be anything to prove that it did not exist earlier; in fact, all the evidence that we now have in favour of its having existed earlier, we should then have.' Of course he hastened to add: '. . . we are none of us prepared for a moment to entertain the supposition that the world began five minutes ago.'[2] In saying this, Bertrand Russell is approaching the attitude of the modern philosopher that any train of thought which produces a result at variance with common sense should not be considered. (In modern philosophy it is always necessary to conclude that common sense is right. If you know the conclusion which is desired to any given intellectual problem, it makes it much easier to get there.)

*

Consider these remarks by Jung:

> If there is something we cannot know, we must necessarily abandon it as an intellectual problem. For example, I do not know for what reason the universe has come into being, and shall never know. Therefore I must drop this question as a scientific or intellectual problem.[3]

This is, of course, not the best kind of modern thinking. It is too clearly stated. Jung could have rendered his position impregnable by hinting obscurely at his position, as at something too profound for mere verbalisation, and at the same time so well-known to all right-thinking persons as to make utterance super-

[1] *An Enquiry Concerning Human Understanding*, Section IV, Part II, quoted in *The Empiricists*, Doubleday, New York, 1961, p. 332.
[2] *Human Knowledge, Its Scope and Limits*, Allen & Unwin, London 1948, p. 228.
[3] C. G. Jung, *Memories, Dreams, Reflections*, Collins and Routledge & Kegan Paul, London, 1963, p. 280.

fluous. But since, on this occasion, Jung expressed himself with unwonted clarity, it is possible to disagree.

In the first place, how can Jung possibly be sure that he can never know for what reason the universe has come into being ? To have read the sceptical philosophers should surely lead to a realisation that one is in a state of total uncertainty. At any moment one must say that one seems to remember a certain past; but how can one delimit what the future mutations of one's consciousness might be ?

To say that one can never know something is a statement that can only be applied, and that by courtesy, to situations which depend on factors where probabilistic assessment is possible. So we might say: I am told that there is a certain book in Tibet of which there is only one copy, and the probability that my source of information about this is correct is very high. I am determined never to go to Tibet, so I am sure that I shall never know what is in this book.

But although we may choose to regard the ultimate uncertainty as irrelevant to answering questions about our everyday lives— for example, we may consult the railway timetable without paying too much attention to the consideration that we may be being hallucinated about the figures on the page—it is quite inappropriate to leave the ultimate uncertainty out in dealing with ultimate questions.

It is absolutely impossible for anyone to make the slightest assessment of the probability that he will ever know the reason for existence.

Also, there is no logical connection between 'I believe that I shall never be able to find an answer to this question' and 'therefore I must stop thinking about this question in a rational manner.' The connection is a psychological, not a logical, one, and it would be impossible to make it if other psychological factors were not present. For example, a person might think: 'I cannot bear not knowing why the universe is there. If I do not think about it I shall go mad. So I prefer to think about it, whether or not I think it probable that my thinking will ever arrive at a conclusion.'

It follows that Jung's remarks are only compatible with the psychological premiss: 'I am not very interested in the facts of the situation, and can easily find alternative activities to thinking about it.'

This may serve to illustrate why old-fashioned philosophy was plainly undesirable, since a study of it might produce analytical habits of thought.

*

In understanding modern philosophy an illuminating philosopher to consider is George Moore. He had all the correct modern attitudes; it is just that he expressed them too explicitly. Linguistic philosophy has developed vastly improved techniques for arriving at identical conclusions by means of verbal sequences so complicated and obscure that it is difficult to accuse it of having arrived at them.

Moore's articles frequently had appealing titles, such as 'A Defence of Common-Sense', and 'The Proof of an External World'. Moore's position is that he knows with certainty that the common sense view of the world is true. He knows that there is an external world, and living human beings with whom he can communicate. Criticising Hume, he proceeds as follows: 'if Hume's principles were true, I could never know that this pencil exists, but I do know that this pencil exists, and therefore Hume's arguments cannot be true.'[1] In 'The Proof of an External World' he writes: 'I can prove now, for instance, that two human hands exist. How? By holding up my two hands, and saying, as I make a certain gesture with the right hand, "Here is one hand", and adding, as I make a certain gesture with the left, "and here is the other".'[2]

Moore may not have had the best possible technique for making sure that everything he said was incomprehensible except to specialists, but his evident desire to defend the common sense view of the world illustrates the dilemma in which the intellectual world felt itself to be as it entered the present century. Moore was a great influence on a generation of Cambridge philosophers, and may be held to have contributed greatly to the decline of philosophy.

However, as already remarked, the sentences by Moore and Jung which we have quoted are not quite of the best quality. It is curious that an age whose philosophers are allegedly dedicated to the most rigorously restrictive use of words should express its most basic dogmas in verbal forms which are totally meaningless.

[1] Quoted in John Passmore, *A Hundred Years of Philosophy*, Gerald Duckworth, London, 1957, p. 213.
[2] *Ibid.*, p. 213.

Consider, for example, this very typical statement of the position of modern theology.

> Nowadays many theologians consider that God cannot be conceived of as distinct from the actual process of being itself. The God of evolution *is* evolution itself, and evolves with it.'[1]

How on earth, one may wonder, can evolution evolve with itself? Does it perhaps mean that the cause of evolution is not separate from evolution? Evolution is caused by itself, and evolves with itself?

As a matter of fact, what is really meant by this and many similar statements is: 'We do not like thinking about the situation in which we find ourselves in any way that reminds us how little we know about it, or provides the slightest stimulus to intellectual activity. There is no need to do so.' The assertion that an abstract concept is identical with a concrete one is very modern, and occurs in many fields of modern thought. It is easy to induce a modern philosopher to say such things as: 'The events between now and next Thursday do not take time, they are time.' Intellectually, of course, this makes no sense at all, but it sounds obscure, may justifiably claim to be difficult to understand, and prevents any further discussion of unpleasantly abstract ideas by pinning our attention firmly back on the concrete world of common sense.

These assertions that one thing (more abstract) *is* another thing (more concrete) reflect the desire to abolish all considerations which might provide a contrast or alternative to the common sense view of the world, resting on social agreement. This is, indeed, apparent even in the two typical examples already given: time *is* the succession of events; God *is* evolution. The psychological outlook underlying such assertions is even more transparently obvious in assertions such as Sartre's that a man's genius *is* the books he has written, and in Adler's that an unrecognised genius is impossible, since a genius is the person who most benefits mankind. (This precludes any possibility of defining a genius in any other way—as, for example, a person of high ability; and it also assumes that a state of perfect identity exists between what benefits mankind and what mankind is prepared to recognise as benefiting it.)

*

[1] Peter Lewis, *Daily Mail*, reviewing *The Biology of God* by Sir Alister Hardy, 17 July 1975.

A characteristic of the remarks we have quoted from Moore and Jung is that it is possible to disagree with them because you can see what they are saying. The utterances of modern thinkers stimulate neither agreement nor disagreement in the same way, and certainly do not suggest trains of analytical thought. They are designed to stun and daze the stupefied mind into a socially acceptable position, by referring endlessly and implicitly to underlying assumptions which can never be stated. Any single sentence taken on its own is virtually meaningless; so in fact is any combination of sentences, however large, but you get the stunning effect which is intended.

For example, in *The Death of the Family* we find:

> If we talk about an instinctual urge to have a good feed we are talking about something that comes from nothing. Something may come from nothing if the nothing is a particular nothing. In this case the particularity of the nothing is the line of its circumscription by the world as an absence, lack, what is not there. The world here includes certain edible objects; the distance and obstacles between us and the objects, and our bodies as objects in the world that can be observed by others; the hunger contractions in our stomachs; the neuro-chemical alterations in the hunger state that can be recorded; and so on. It's a bit like running one's finger across a table and then letting it drop off into nothing at the edge. The edge is neither the table nor is it the 'nothing' one's finger drops into, but both the table, which is something, and the nothing, which is not, define the edge as non-existent but as a specific non-existence. If we can extend our metaphysical imagination to the point of desubstantializing our finger so that it becomes a non-finger we get closer to what an instinct 'is'.[1]

If you find yourself uncomfortably bemused, you may like to know that what is conveyed to my mind by that passage is: 'The modern mind finds it very uncomfortable to think about psychological entities, conscious or unconscious, because they suggest that there may be things inside people which are not totally under the control of what society can do to them. On the other hand, it is convenient to talk about depth psychology and instinctual urges, as in this way we can make out that everyone is pretty much the same and extremely degraded. This situation is resolved by presenting the discussion of psychology as so fantastically difficult that no one will think it is something they can think about for them-

[1] David Cooper, *The Death of the Family*, Penguin, 1971, p. 33.

selves; they will think they must find some socially accredited expert who can teach them how to talk about it correctly without making sense.'

Modern thought, as has been said, stuns by implication, and this confidence of finality is at its most outrageous in the dogmatism implicit in modern science. What has already been said of psychology is true of modern physics and philosophy as well—you must find a socially accredited expert to teach you how to talk about them correctly without making sense. This covers a large number of danger areas.[1]

[1] For a further discussion of modern philosophy see my book *The Human Evasion*, Chapter 9 ('The Philosophy of Evasion').

CHAPTER 6

The Decline and Fall of Physics

IT should not be thought that the emotional resistances of the human race only affect its attitudes towards research of an obviously innovating kind. In accepted fields of science also, prejudice strongly affects what may be thought about and what may be thought about it. To illustrate this, let us consider theoretical physics, which indeed might be thought to be poised as dangerously as parapsychology on the brink of intolerable ideas. Another reason for associating theoretical physics and parapsychology is that when genuine solutions to the present problems are found in either field, they may well affect the other. Eventually we must account for telepathy, precognition and psychokinesis in mathematical terms, and relate them to forms of energy operating in space and time. The fact that they do not fit very well with a common-sense three-dimensional space, and with electromagnetic radiation operating within it, leads us to consider those extensions of its intellectual scope which physics has been holding at bay for the past century.

Physics has never been a comfortable subject for human psychology. The desire to regard everything outside the human race's purview as insignificant, and everything within that purview as firmly under the control of tribal myth and custom, is as strong today as it was in the time of Galileo. Although the laws of astronomy came to be accepted, I do not see that human psychology can ever have been entirely happy with the idea of an infinite universe. It does not seem to me that there is anything in the life of the average man, even of the modern intellectual man, which would not go on just as well, and perhaps a little more comfortably, if tribal custom happened to dictate belief in an inverted bowl overhead.

The human race, in fact, did not have to live with the totally undiluted idea of an infinite universe for very long. There came to be an idea, which must have been found soothing, that in some incomprehensible fashion the universe might be finite (in a sense) after all. This relaxing idea was in fact, as we shall see later, expounded with the utmost confusion, since it rested upon the idea of curvature, and this concealed an idea which was not agreeable at all—that of higher dimensionality.

Now the idea of higher dimensionality is one which the human race has always known should not be thought about. For example, the development of mathematics was held up at one time, because the ancient Greek mathematicians did not have algebra, and treated problems that we would regard as part of algebra by geometrical methods. Thus the square of a number was represented, quite literally, by a square, and Euclid arrives at what we would call the solutions to a quadratic equation by a construction involving figures of equal area (Euclid, VI, 28). In consequence, when algebra did start to be developed, equations of degree higher than the third were avoided as being 'imaginary', or 'against nature'. Again Möbius, in discussing the geometrical fact that an object could be made to coincide with its reflection in a plane-mirror if there were a space of four dimensions, says, 'Da aber ein solcher Raum nicht gedacht werden kann, so ist auch die Coincidenz in diesem Falle unmöglich.'[1] ('As such a space cannot be imagined, therefore it is impossible that they could be made to coincide in this case.') The reason for this aversion is clear, and it is exactly the same as for people's aversion to Galileo's idea of the earth going round the sun. The human race has a kind of agoraphobia. It does not like to be surrounded by too many possibilities it does not know about, and by too much space in which to put them.

On examining modern theoretical physics we find, in fact, the most extraordinary state of affairs. While physicists may be heard to murmur that it is rather boring to be a physicist in this century, when there is nothing left of much importance to be discovered, the whole subject is in an amazingly incoherent state. On closer examination, one is surprised to find in how many places the obvious thought that presents itself to the mind is one about higher dimensionality, and that this is of course not mentioned at all.

[1] Quoted in *Geometry of Four Dimensions* by H. P. Manning, Dover Books, 1956, p. 4 *n.*, first published in 1914.

The fact is that physics could not develop far without being confronted by certain paradoxes which were first apparent in the last century in the study of electromagnetic theory. To these were added the various phenomena which suggested the curvature of our space, and to these again the extraordinary goings-on in particle physics, in which, as everybody knows, paradoxical happenings are the order of the day.

In this situation it was clear that our ordinary thinking, based on what we could readily imagine as a result of our experience in a three-dimensional world, was not adequate. There are, however, two ways of reacting to this. You can try to extend your system of concepts by presenting to yourself as best you can how things would have to happen in higher space—and, of course, by extending the concepts you have in other ways. Or you can do what physicists have in fact done, which is to rely more and more on mathematical formulations divorced from conceptual understanding, while muddling themselves into ascribing to these mathematical formulations a status as the objects of dogmatic belief to which they are in no way entitled. While the human race has always had an immense tendency towards dogmatic belief, in the present context this has certainly owed a good deal to the inconvenient proximity of ideas about higher dimensionality. (I may say I am aware of the contexts in which higher dimensionality does appear to be invoked as a mathematical convenience. This does not affect the point I am making, that it has not been thought about.) In fact, I suspect that the whole fabric of modern physics (and fabric is probably not the right word for a set of patches strung together with a few loose stitches) may be regarded as an attempt to avoid higher dimensionality.

Let us consider some of the contexts in which it would appear most obvious to refer explicitly to higher dimensionality, and where this reference is virtually always omitted.

A good deal of importance is attached in modern physics to something called parity, and the conservation or otherwise of this. When I say that importance is attached, I do not of course mean that it is ever explained why it should be thought important, or that statements are made about lines of thought which might be suggested by the fact that it has been shown not to be conserved.

Now, in fact, the question about conservation or otherwise of parity is really this. If we reflect in a mirror any set of physical events that can happen in our space, does the picture we get always correspond to another set of events that could also happen according to the physical laws of our space? That this is a significant question becomes somewhat more apparent when it is pointed out that a reflection in a mirror is the same thing as a rotation about a plane. A rotation about a plane is the characteristic form of rotation in four-dimensional space, in the same way that rotation about a line is the characteristic form of rotation in a three-dimensional space. (Rotation about a plane is, of course, inconceivable to us. That is no reason why it should not happen.)

Now one of the first symptoms one may notice of the curious state of modern physics is that, although reflections in mirrors are frequently discussed, and more mathematical representations of the same idea even more so, it is never pointed out that what is being discussed is the question of rotating the physical system in 'higher space'. This is very odd, because the first and most immediate association of ideas with reflection in a mirror is the concept of rotation about a plane.

In the light of this association, the emotional loading attached to parity conservation becomes more obvious. We already know that our laws of physics work all ways on in three-dimensional space as observed by us. They might not have done. There might have been a 'down' direction governing certain phenomena which applied for the whole universe. To give an analogy in fewer dimensions which may make the idea clearer, if some beings were living in a two-dimensional plane, which was held vertically in the earth's gravitational field, all their doings would be governed by this gravitational field which had a unique, but to them quite arbitrary, direction at all points in their space. However, until parity was found not to be conserved, there were no signs of any such orientation effects in the physical laws of our three-dimensional universe. This meant that, so far as we could see, our space was not subject to influences which depended upon its orientation in higher space.

But when we ask the question whether all our physical laws will still hold good if they are reflected in a mirror, we are asking a question analogous to that which our plane beings might ask in imagining whether all their laws of physics held good on both sides of the plane. To turn over a section of a plane within a plane is something which can only be done by taking it temporarily out of the plane into three-dimensional space, and when it is put back its sides are reversed relative to three-dimensional space. The analogous operation to this in three-dimensional space is, so to speak, to turn over a section of the three-space, which can only be done by moving it temporarily through four-space. When it is put back in three-space, its 'sides' have been reversed relative to four-space. (It should be borne in mind that a three-space is a surface in higher space, and a line passing through it in four-space from one side to the other cuts it in one point only.)

To return to our plane beings; if all their laws of physics did not hold good without alteration for a section of their plane when it was turned over and put back, it would suggest that their space was, in this respect also, influenced by the state of affairs in the higher space surrounding it. For example, the sun might be shining on one side of this plane world, so that one side was lighted and the other in shadow. If we find that any of our laws of physics become different when we reflect them in a mirror (or rotate them about a plane) this must suggest that what goes on in our space is influenced by its orientation in higher space.

In fact, the decline of physics began with the formulation of the laws of electromagnetism in the last century. The paradoxes inherent in this formulation were never recognised, even by those who formulated them. The tendency had already begun to produce elegant and sophisticated mathematical formulations based on a hopelessly shaky conceptual foundation. As a matter of fact, the paradoxes of electromagnetism already suggested that parity might not be conserved.

*

There is a remarkable similarity of psychological structure between modern physics and modern philosophy. To appreciate this, it is only necessary to read George Moore's description of Wittgenstein bashfully hinting at the potency of his indescribable method in eliminating all difficulties after sufficiently prolonged and mysterious studies, with the remarks of Feynman addressed to the neophyte in physics referring to the indescribable course of mental evolution that lies ahead of him as he becomes able to understand, without of course understanding.

> I was a good deal surprised by some of the things he said about the difference between 'philosophy' in the sense in which what he was

doing might be called 'philosophy' (he called this 'modern philosophy'), and what has traditionally been called 'philosophy'. He said
that what he was doing was a 'new subject', and not merely a stage
in a 'continuous development'; that there was now, in philosophy, a
'kink' in the 'development of human thought', comparable to that
which occurred when Galileo and his contemporaries invented
dynamics; that a 'new method' had been discovered, as had happened
when 'chemistry was developed out of alchemy'; and that it was now
possible for the first time that there should be 'skilful' philosophers,
though of course there had in the past been 'great' philosophers.

He went on to say that, though philosophy had now been 'reduced
to a matter of skill', yet this skill, like other skills, is very difficult to
acquire. One difficulty was that it required a 'sort of thinking' to
which we are not accustomed and to which we have not been
trained — a sort of thinking very different from what is required in
the sciences. And he said that the required skill could not be acquired
merely by hearing lectures: discussion was essential. As regards his
own work, he said it did not matter whether his results were true or
not: what mattered was that 'a method had been found'.

In answer to the question why this 'new subject' should be called
'philosophy' he said in (III) that though what he was doing was
certainly different from what, e.g., Plato or Berkeley had done, yet
people might feel that it 'takes the place of' what they had done —
might be inclined to say 'This is what I really wanted' and to identify
it with what they had done, though it is really different, just as (as I
said above, pages 304–5) a person who had been trying to trisect an
angle by rule and compasses might, when shown the proof that this is
impossible, be inclined to say that this impossible thing was the very
thing he had been trying to do, though what he had been trying to do
was really different. But in (II) he had also said that the 'new subject'
did really resemble what had been traditionally called 'philosophy'
in the three respects that (1) it was very general, (2) it was fundamental both to ordinary life and to the sciences, and (3) it was independent of any special results of science; that therefore the
application to it of the word 'philosophy' was not purely arbitrary.

He did not expressly try to tell us exactly what the 'new method'
which had been found was. But he gave some hints as to its nature.
He said, in (II), that the 'new subject' consisted in 'something like
putting in order our notions as to what can be said about the world',
and compared this to the tidying up of a room where you have to
move the same object several times before you can get the room really
tidy. He also said that we were 'in a muddle about things', which we
had to try to clear up; that we had to follow a certain instinct which
leads us to ask certain questions, though we don't even understand
what these questions mean; that our asking them results from 'a
vague mental uneasiness', like that which leads children to ask
'Why?'; and that this uneasiness can be cured 'either by showing
that a particular question is not permitted, or by answering it'.

(G. E. Moore, 'Wittgenstein's Lectures in 1930–33', *Mind*, Vol. LXIV, 1955; reprinted in *Philosophical Papers*, Allen & Unwin, London, 1959, pp. 322–3.)

In the last chapter we described how in quantum mechanics the angular momentum of a thing does not have an arbitrary direction, but its component along a given axis can take on only certain equally spaced, discrete values. It is a shocking and peculiar thing. You may think that perhaps we should not go into such things until your minds are more advanced and ready to accept this kind of an idea. Actually, your minds will never become more advanced—in the sense of being able to accept such a thing easily. There isn't any descriptive way of making it intelligible that isn't so subtle and advanced in its own form that it is more complicated than the thing you were trying to explain. The behaviour of matter on a small scale —as we have remarked many times—is different from anything that you are used to and is very strange indeed. As we proceed with classical physics, it is a good idea to get a growing acquaintance with the behavior of things on a small scale, at first as a kind of experience without any deep understanding. Understanding of these matters comes very slowly, if at all. Of course, one does get better able to know what is going to happen in a quantum-mechanical situation— if that is what understanding means—but one never gets a comfortable feeling that these quantum-mechanical rules are 'natural'. Of course they *are*, but they are not natural to our own experience at an ordinary level. We should explain that the attitude that we are going to take with regard to this rule about angular momentum is quite different from many of the other things we have talked about. We are not going to try to 'explain' it, but we must at least *tell* you what happens; it would be dishonest to describe the magnetic properties of materials without mentioning the fact that the classical description of magnetism—of angular momentum and magnetic moments—is incorrect. (Richard P. Feynman, *The Feynman Lectures on Physics*, Addison-Wesley, 1965, Vol. II, p. 35–1.)

In philosophy, as we know, the seemingly meticulous study of words and their functions is used to conceal what is actually going on. In modern physics an equally earnest and obsessional attention to the precise functions of clocks and measuring rods is used to conceal what it is really all being about. This, at any rate, is the case with the relativistic part of things. Einstein was really a forerunner of the great modern tendency not to let anyone know what are the issues really involved. Einstein's work is therefore partially comprehensible (or at least, the points at which it does not make sense may be located without too much difficulty). This is, as we have already pointed out in other contexts, a characteristic only of modern thought of less than the finest maturity, in which it is impossible to find out exactly where it does not make sense, because it is impossible to find anywhere it does.

The fixation of modern philosophy on the use of words and of physics on measuring rods and mathematical equations reflects the universal shift of attention in modern thought from the matter in hand to the social rules for dealing with it. Everyone has become more interested in training than in ability, in qualifications than efficiency, in the way in which things ought to be done in accordance with socialist principles than in whether there is any possibility of anything getting done in such a way.

The chief difficulty of modern theoretical physics resides not in the fact that it expresses itself almost exclusively in mathematical symbols, but in the psychological difficulty of supposing that complete nonsense can be seriously promulgated and transmitted by persons who have sufficient intelligence of some kind to perform operations in differential and integral calculus quite neatly. However, when one considers what the human race is capable of in contexts in which it is not expressing itself in mathematical symbolism, such as in philosophy, this difficulty evaporates. In this sense, an awareness of the procedures of modern linguistic philosophy may actually be of considerable assistance in penetrating the true meaning of modern physics.

*

In physics modern thought reached its finest development in the quantum theory (which is not a theory) and in which the function of clocks and measuring rods is taken over by mathematical equations. We are exhorted most earnestly and explicitly not to think, but to keep our attention firmly fixed on these equations, as the would-be linguistic philosopher is urged to attend firmly and exclusively to the functions of words in linguistic usage. For example:

> The fact that wave functions are complex functions should not be considered a weak point of the quantum mechanical theory. Actually, it is a desirable feature because it makes it immediately obvious that we should not attempt to attribute to wave functions a physical existence in the same sense that water waves have a physical existence. That is, we should not try to answer, or even pose, the questions: Exactly what is waving, and what is it waving in? (R. M. Eisberg, *Fundamentals of Modern Physics*, Wiley, New York, 1961, p. 171.)

This example is particularly instructive since it not only so clearly expresses the desire to eliminate thought, but also reveals that the thought being avoided might, as in this instance, tend to lead to considerations of higher dimensional space. If we allow ourselves to entertain the idea of four-dimensional space and of the forms of wave motion which are possible in it, it is quite easy to think of a number of situations that might give rise to a wave equation containing a complex variable.

Exhortations on no account to confuse yourself by thinking occur throughout expositions of quantum theory, and the student is provided with every practical inducement not to do so, as the writers of textbooks in this area prefer to express themselves in mathematical equations with, if possible (and you would be surprised how often it is possible), no indication at all of what the equations refer to.

At the same time, modern physics is not averse to cooking up an aura of profound metaphysical mystification where there is no need for it at all. This, again, is paralleled in modern philosophy in which, as we have already pointed out, nothing is so laudable as that obscurity of utterance which arises from dishonesty.

> The result of an experiment is not determined, as it would be according to classical ideas, by the conditions under the control of the experimenter. The most that can be predicted is a set of possible results, with a probability of occurrence for each.
>
> The foregoing discussion about the result of an experiment with a single obliquely polarised photon incident on a crystal of tourmaline answers all that can legitimately be asked about what happens to an obliquely polarised photon when it reaches the tourmaline. Questions about what decides whether the photon is to go through or not and how it changes its direction of polarisation when it does go through cannot be investigated by experiment and should be regarded as outside the domain of science. Nevertheless some further description is necessary in order to correlate the results of this experiment with the results of other experiments that might be performed with photons and to fit them all into a general scheme. Such further description should be regarded, not as an attempt to answer questions outside the domain of science, but as an aid to the formulation of rules for expressing concisely the results of large numbers of experiments. (P. A. M. Dirac, *The Principles of Quantum Mechanics*, Oxford University Press, 1958, p. 6.)

This is, of course, nonsense. There is no logical reason why you *should* regard the results of your experiments as all that can ever be found out. All this illustrates is the strange tendency on the part of the human mind, very apparent also in philosophy, to arrive at dogmatic statements about the situation, at the same time incidentally eliminating any possibility of uncomfortable thoughts. It is curious that the human mind is so seldom content to consider a number of different ways of viewing a situation as *possible* but none of them as morally obligatory. We may indeed observe, as Dirac points out, that the most we can predict *at present* is a set of possible results, with a probability of occurrence for each. Questions about what decides whether the photon is to go through or not cannot *at present* be investigated by experiment. That is no reason for regarding them as outside the domain of science, except on a very modern and arbitrary definition of science. Even if human science never, at any time in the future, devises any means for the experimental investigation of these questions, this will not mean that they do not possess answers, and it will not mean that it is impossible to think about possible answers, and to consider on purely intellectual grounds the relative attractions of the various possibilities.

It is, contrary to popular belief, perfectly possible to be aware of the experimental results produced by physics, and of the limitations in various respects of those results, and also of the mathematical formulae employed in quantum mechanics, without feeling any necessity to stop thinking. Certainly it is desirable to be aware that one's experimental results prove no more than they do, but one of the things that an experimental result or even a mathematical equation can never prove, is that speculative and analytical thought is useless, still more that it is morally wrong.

Certainly one may observe in a given situation that, while one cannot give an intellectually satisfactory account of what is going on, one is in the position of being able to make predictions on a probabilistic basis. It is right and proper that one should make as much use as possible of the probabilistic inferences one is able to make. But this is no reason at all for saying that science is about probabilities, and that thinking what explanations are possible for the probabilistic results one observes is an unscientific kind of thinking.

*

A priceless example of gratuitous mystification is provided by the introduction, in standard textbooks of quantum mechanics, of the notion of *operators*.

We are talking about a particle and its associated wave function. (Do not ask how it is associated, or what the wave function is.) After some pages, we find something which indicates 'that there is an association between the dynamical quantity p [momentum] and the *differential operator* $-i\hbar\,\delta/\delta x$. A similar association between the dynamical quantity E [energy] and the differential operator $i\hbar\,\delta/\delta t$ can be found.'[1]

We then make the suggestion that we can replace the quantities p and E by their 'associated differential operators' in order to obtain 'operator equations'. I know that this sounds very obscure, but it isn't really; it is just the least natural way of approaching the matter, and there are good reasons for it.

We then 'postulate associations' between p and E and their 'associated operators', the mysteriousness of which we emphasise by using a little double arrow to indicate them, thus:

$$p \leftrightarrow -i\hbar\,\frac{\delta}{\delta x}$$

$$E \leftrightarrow i\hbar\,\frac{\delta}{\delta t}$$

If I may now give a simple example to illustrate what has just been being said, the reasons for this mystification may become more apparent.

If we take the kinetic energy of a particle in normal space, $\frac{1}{2}mv^2$ (which we could, if we wished, denote mysteriously by ψ), it may be observed that whenever we multiply $\frac{1}{2}mv^2$ by $2/v^2$ the result is m (mass). We might then say that the mass of the particle is *associated* with the operator $2/v^2$ and we might denote this association by an evocative little double arrow, thus:

$$m \leftrightarrow \frac{2}{v^2}$$

This really has a considerable air of impenetrable profundity and unobviousness. If, however, the exposition of the concept of operators in quantum mechanics were given so directly, it would naturally lead to the questions of exactly what the wave function

[1] R. M. Eisberg, *Fundamentals of Modern Physics*, p. 203.

represents, and why operating on it in certain simple mathematical ways should produce certain results. It is better to refer to an 'association' as if we were dealing with a matter of metaphysical difficulty. I have even seen it suggested that if something is always associated with an operator by means of a little double arrow, there is in some sense a kind of identity between them, so that, for example, the operator $i\hbar\ \delta/\delta t$ is in some sense the energy of the particle. (The reader will remember that time *is* the succession of events, and God *is* evolution. This technique is always used to eliminate abstract thought; in the present example its function is to focus attention mesmerically upon mathematical formulae.)

A somewhat similar haste to arrive at a dogmatic and acceptable conclusion may be seen in the modern method for eliminating Mach's shock. According to the story, Mach tells how he received this intellectual shock when he learned, as a boy, of Oersted's rule for the behaviour of a compass needle close to an electric current. If the current in a straight wire is flowing in one direction, the compass needle points right, perpendicularly to the wire, but if it flows in the other direction, the needle points left. But it appears arbitrary that the needle should turn one way rather than the other. If the experiment were reflected in a mirror, the result would be a situation that does not occur in nature. Thus, if the needle pointed right when the current flowed in one direction, in the reflection the current would flow in the same direction but the needle would point left.

It is alleged that a deeper understanding of magnetism shows that the asymmetry in the situation is only apparent. A magnet is a magnet because it contains electrons making loop motions. If they are reflected in a mirror, the loops go the other way and the polarity of the magnet changes. Therefore, what was its north pole becomes, on reflection, its south pole, and vice versa.

Or, to put it another way, since in our space we only encounter electric charges and no magnetic charges, the only devices which we can use to test the direction of a magnetic field are those which depend on the presence of electric charge. If we decide that electric charge is a real entity and reflect it in our mirror, but we decide that magnetic field lines are not real and are not to be reflected, but drawn in to our reflected picture of electric charges to suit ourselves, it is true that we can arrange for our laws of electromagnetism to be reflected in a mirror without alteration. But it appears to me that this is merely a possible way of regarding the matter, and not one that we can be certain is correct. Modern physicists have, of course, no feeling that the status of physical events is something that has to be found out, and about which they can make only tentative suggestions. When the socially acceptable solution is obvious, as it is here, they proceed without scruple to instant dogmatism.

Modern physicists are curiously concerned to make laws for mirror reflections, no matter how complicated and arbitrary, which will leave physical laws unchanged. Some explanation for this obsession may be provided by the remarks already made on the relationship between reflection in a mirror and rotation about a plane in higher space. However, I find it difficult to see how they find their conclusions about matter and anti-matter comforting.

'. . . if one performs a mirror reflection *and* converts all matter into antimatter, then physical laws remain unchanged. This combined transformation which leaves physical laws unchanged could thus be *defined* as the true mirror reflection process. According to this definition, mirror reflection symmetry is restored.'[1] The price of restoring this symmetry is thus to admit that antimatter is what ordinary matter turns into on being rotated about a plane. Since I thought the object of the whole exercise was to eliminate explicit recognition of the fact that anything might ever be rotated about a plane in higher space, this seems a high price to pay for symmetry.

Incidentally, *à propos* this question of how readily it might present itself to the mind that particles whose properties were all precise numerical representations of one another in all but the interchange of a few positive and negative signs were really the same particle rotated in higher space, I must admit I find it strange that the presence in nature of positive-negative pairs of things, such as positive and negative electric charges, precisely equal in magnitude but opposite in sign, has never given rise to discussion whether these pairs are not actually manifestations of the same thing oriented differently with regard to our three-dimensional space. In this connection, it is interesting to bear in mind that a line, passing through our three-dimensional space from one side of it (in higher space) to the other side of it, would cut it in a point.

This consideration, as a matter of fact, has some relevance to the

[1] C. N. Yang, *Elementary Particles*, Princeton University Press, 1962, p. 59.

wave-particle problem. The reader may remember that it is supposed to be the most convincing proof possible of the absurdity and naiveté of continuing to think, that particles in our three-dimensional space are observed to behave with properties which in some ways resemble those of three-dimensional particles, and in some ways resemble those of waves in three-dimensional space.

The consideration of the forms of wave motion possible in higher space, and of the ways in which such waves might intersect a three-dimensional space, provides a fairly wide selection of possibilities which may be compared with the observed experimental facts.

★

Another example of quite unnecessary obscurity may be found in Eddington's discussion of the notion of the curvature of space-time. This is, of course, yet another example of pre-modern thought, in which what is being evaded is still relatively easy to discern.

> In water of ordinary density the curvature is the same as that of space in the form of a sphere of radius 570,000,000 kilometres. . . . So far as I can make out a homogeneous mass of water of about this size (and no larger) could exist. It would have no centre, and no boundary, every point of it being in the same position with respect to the whole mass as every other point of it—like points on the *surface* of a sphere with respect to the surface. Any ray of light after travelling for an hour or two would come back to the starting point. Nothing could enter or leave the mass, because there is no boundary to enter or leave by; in fact, it is coextensive with space. There could not be any other world anywhere else, because there isn't an 'anywhere else'. (Sir Arthur Eddington, *Space, Time and Gravitation*. Cambridge University Press, 1959, p. 148.)

As a matter of fact, of course, there is an enormous amount of 'anywhere else'. It is impossible to bend a line without implying the existence of a two-dimensional space; it is impossible to bend a plane unless you have a three-dimensional space to put it in; and it is impossible to bend a three- or four-dimensional entity (whether or not one of the dimensions involved is called time) without implying the existence of a four- or five-dimensional continuum respectively.

One might as well say that when one had painted the surface of a tennis ball red there was no more space in the universe where red paint could be put.

Incidentally, we may note in passing everyone's predilection for discussing the curvature of space-time. The psychological motivation behind this is of course the desire to avoid discussing clearly the curvature of *space*, and the question of higher dimensionality in general.

I know that Eddington is no longer fashionable. However, it can hardly be counted to the credit of modern physics that it is almost impossible to quote any absurd statements by a really modern writer about the curvature of space, or indeed of space-time. The absurdity resides in the fact that no statements are made. Certainly some pages of mathematical symbolism may be discovered where the absence of verbal statements is hilarious, if you find human dishonesty entertaining. But a taste for this form of humour is, perhaps, a little esoteric.[1]

---

[1] For a further discussion of modern physics, see my book *The Human Evasion*, Chapter X ('The Science of Evasion').

CHAPTER 7

The Decline and Fall of Medicine

A LINE of research which rapidly became unpopular, at least in so far as carrying it any further was concerned, was that associated with the study of the extension of mental control of physiological functions. This was no doubt because it was soon perceived that it was going to suit the book of the twentieth century much better to concentrate on the power of the physiological to control mental functions, rather than the other way round. However, in the early days of psychology and psychical research, striking observations were made which showed that physiological functions could, at times and under certain conditions, be consciously or at any rate mentally controlled to a much greater extent than normal experience would lead one to suppose.

It is not now realised to how great an extent knowledge of the phenomenon of hypnosis was developed by members of the early Society for Psychical Research, and in particular by Gurney, who went to the rather extreme lengths of taking a medical degree in the interests of his researches. The somewhat uncynical respect for socially approved training courses evinced by this action was perhaps, in part, responsible for the rapid termination of research into hypnosis. Gurney and the other members of the Society for Psychical Research felt, with great social conscientiousness, that hypnosis was rightly the concern of the medical profession, and having developed knowledge of the phenomenon to a certain point they dutifully handed it over, so to speak. The medical profession, of course, dropped it like a hot brick, and no significant developments have been made in knowledge of the phenomenon, nor has it been developed as a method of treatment.

One isolated experiment carried out by a doctor may be mentioned, as indicative of the potentialities which have not been developed. The case concerns a boy of 16 suffering from congenital ichthyosis (erythroderma ichthyosiforme), a rare disease in which the skin becomes progressively thickened from birth, until it becomes black and scaly, and so inelastic that any attempt to bend results in a crack in the surface, causing a wound. The whole of this subject's skin was covered by this black, horny layer except for the chest, neck and face. In this condition it was almost impossible for him to engage in any sort of activity whatsoever, because any movement of hands or legs opened up wounds which became infected. Thus he had been unable to attend school, or to take up any job. The cause of the condition is unknown, except that it is thought to be congenital, and there is no known method of treatment. Skin grafting had been tried without success, the grafts suffering the same change as the already affected skin. After the failure of the skin graft, hypnosis was tried:

> On February 10, 1951, the patient was hypnotised and, under hypnosis, suggestion was made that the left arm would clear. (The suggestion was limited to the left arm, so as to exclude the possibility of spontaneous resolution.)
> About five days later the horny layer softened, became friable, and fell off. The skin underneath was slightly erythematous, but normal in texture and colour. From a black and armour-like casing, the skin became pink and soft within a few days. Improvement occurred first in the flexures and areas of friction, and later on the rest of the arm. The erythema faded in a few days. At the end of 10 days the arm was completely clear from shoulder to wrist. (A. A. Mason, 'Ichthyosis Treated by Hypnosis', *British Medical Journal*, 1952, pp. 422-3.)

The other arm was later cleared in the same way, and almost complete success was met on giving suggestions for the recovery of the rest of his body. The boy was subsequently able to take up a normal life.

In a letter to the British Medical Journal subsequent to the publication of this case, Dr. F. Ray Bettley made the following comment on the implications of this case:

> . . . I had the privilege of seeing the patient when Dr. Mason demonstrated him at the Royal Society of Medicine—and a very impressive demonstration it was—and I think the general reaction, like my own, was of more than surprise; it was fantastic, but true.
> Erythroderma ichthyosiforme is a congenital disorder in which structural abnormality is more important than functional deviation; it is as much an anatomical maldevelopment as is clubfoot. It is

surprising that it should respond to any kind of treatment; that it should respond to hypnotic suggestion demands a revision of current concepts of the relation between mind and body. (*Ibid.*, p. 996.)

Among other phenomena which occur under hypnosis and offer potential lines of research, we may mention the following: lucid dreams,[1] out-of-the-body experiences, extrasensory perception, anaesthesia, and the control of normally autonomic functions, such as body temperature. So little work has been done on many of these phenomena that only isolated observations permit one to recognise their presence as potentialities of the hypnotic state. However, anaesthesia under hypnosis was studied to some extent and it would clearly have been possible to investigate this further with a view to developing it as an alternative to chemical methods of anaesthesia. This, however, would have been too agreeable for the patient, and there is obviously something very appealing in the idea of a human individual reduced, by physical means, to an inert physiology which may then be hacked about *ad lib*.

*

One phenomenon which illustrates the mind's potential for increased control over physiological processes is that of 'skin writing' (dermographia), or the development of marks on the skin of a definite shape. The following is a case investigated by a Dr. Biggs of Lima and quoted by Myers in *Human Personality*:

October 18th, 1885
... Another case ... was the first of this kind of experiment that I tried; it was in Santa Barbara, California. I was staying there in 1879 with a friend, Mr. G., a long-resident chemist in that town. His wife had a kind of half servant and half companion, a girl of about eighteen, who complained to me one day of a pain in her chest. Without her knowing what I intended to do, I tried magnetism; she fell into a deep magnetic sleep in a few minutes. With this subject I tried many interesting experiments, which I will pass over. One day I magnetised her as usual, and told her in a whisper (I had found her to be more susceptible this way than when I spoke aloud in my usual voice), 'You will have a red cross appear on the upper half of your chest, only on every Friday. In the course of some time the words *Sancta* above the cross, and *Crucis* underneath it will appear also; at same

---

[1] For a discussion of lucid dreams occurring under hypnosis, with some examples, see Chapter 18 of my book *Lucid Dreams*, Hamish Hamilton, 1968.

time a little blood will come from the cross.' In my vest pocket I had a cross of rock crystal. I opened the top button of her dress and placed this cross on the upper part of the manubrium, a point she could not see unless by aid of a looking-glass, saying to her, '*This* is the spot where the cross will appear.' This was on a Tuesday. I asked Mrs. G. to watch the girl and tell me if anything seemed to ail her. Next day Mrs. G. told me she had seen the girl now and again put her left wrist over the top part of her chest, over the dress; this was frequently repeated, as if she felt some tickling or slight irritation about the part, but not otherwise noticed; she seemed to carry her hand up now and then unconsciously. When Friday came I said, after breakfast, 'Come, let me magnetise you a little; you have not had a dose for several days.' She was always willing to be magnetised, as she always expressed herself as feeling very much rested and comfortable afterwards. In a few minutes she was in a deep sleep. I unbuttoned the top part of her dress, and there, to my complete and utter astonishment, was a pink cross, exactly over the place where I had put the one of crystal. It appeared every Friday, and was invisible on all other days. This was seen by Mr. and Mrs. G., and my old friend and colleague, Dr. B., who had become much interested in my experiments in magnetism, and often suggested the class of experiments he wished to see tried. About six weeks after the cross first appeared I had occasion to take a trip to the Sandwich Islands. Before going I magnetised the girl, told her that the cross would keep on showing itself every Friday for about four months. I intended my trip to the Islands to last about three months. I did this to save the girl from the infliction of this mark so strangely appearing perhaps for a lifetime, in case anything might happen to me and prevent me from seeing her again. I also asked Dr. B. and Mr. G. to write me by every mail to Honolulu, and tell me if the cross kept on appearing every Friday, and to be very careful to note any change, should any take place, such as the surging of blood or any appearance of the words *Sancta Crucis*. I was rather curious to know if distance between us, the girl and myself, over 2000 miles, made any difference in the apparition of the cross. While I was at the Sandwich Islands I received two letters from Mr. G. and one from Dr. B. by three different mails, each telling that the cross kept on making its appearance as usual; blood had been noticed once, and also part of the letter S above the cross, nothing more. I returned in a little less than three months. The cross still made its appearance every Friday, and did so for about a month more, but getting paler and paler until it became invisible, as nearly as possible four months from the time I left for the Sandwich Islands. The above-mentioned young woman was a native Californian, of Spanish parentage, about eighteen years of age, of tolerably good health, parents and grandparents alive. She was of fair natural intelligence, but utterly ignorant and uneducated . . . M. H. BIGGS, M.D. (F. W. H. Myers, *Human Personality*, Vol. I, pp. 493–4.)

In the case just quoted Dr. Biggs does not indicate whether the cross he observed resembled a raised weal (such as would be caused by a minor burn), or whether the cross was simply a red patch on the skin, caused by an increase in blood flow through the skin blood vessels. The first case in the following passage appears to be an instance of this latter kind:

> In the following case the *intellectual* character, as I have termed it, of the organic process which responds to suggestion is illustrated in a striking and complex way. Mdlle. Ilma S., a subject observed by Drs. Jendrassik and von Krafft-Ebing (mainly at Gratz), was ultimately cured by hypnotic suggestion (or so Dr. Krafft-Ebing claims in 1888) of a lifelong tendency to hysteria and melancholy, such as had driven her grandfather, father, brother, and sister to suicide. She was therefore on the whole a great gainer; but her extreme susceptibility to blistering by suggestion amounted to a real risk in the absence of careful guardianship. Once at least she was much injured and offended by the culpable act of a medical student who laid a pair of scissors upon her chest, telling her that they were red-hot, and thus created a serious wound, which took two months to heal. Krafft-Ebing made a humane variation on this risky experiment. Like Dr. Biggs in the case quoted above, he ordered the production of *red patches* of definite shapes, which were to be formed without itching, pain, or inflammation. The history of the process thus set up is a curious one. The organism had to perform, so to say, a novel feat, which took a great deal longer than the rough and ready process of vesication. From February 24th to May 3rd, 1888, a livid red hyperaemic surface corresponding to the letter K was slowly and painlessly developing itself on a selected and protected area between the shoulder-blades. . . .
>
> But it is the incident next to be cited which speaks the most strongly for the educated character—so to speak—of the intelligence presiding over these organic suggestions.
>
> Mdlle. Ilma S. was permanently anaesthetic on the right side, and that side was therefore, in my view, likely to be more immediately subject to subliminal control. At any rate, it appeared that when any object was pressed on her left side, and suggested as hot, no mark followed at the place of contact; but a corresponding brand appeared, symmetrically and reversed, upon the *right* side. For example, an initial letter, K, was pressed by Dr. Jendrassik on her left shoulder. In a few hours a K-like blister, 'with quite sharp outlines', came on the corresponding spot on the right side. But note that the new K (the letters are figured in Krafft-Ebing's work) was by no means an exact reproduction of the original one. It was of about the same size, but of a different type, in fact, a capital K in another person's handwriting. Just as in Dr. Biggs' cases it was the idea of cruciformity which was induced by suggestion, so here it was the idea of

K-shape; and insomuch as this suggested mark corresponded to an intellectual idea, that idea underwent some idiosyncratic modification in the subject's subliminal intelligence, and the resultant mark, though identical in significance, was different in contour. (*Ibid.* pp. 495–6.)

The following is an example of a similar kind that was investigated by the Institute of Psychophysical Research in Oxford. The pattern on the subject's skin appeared spontaneously in this instance, and not as a result of hypnotic suggestion.

> I had been attending a very boring conference abroad. On my return to England I found that I had on my forehead a small red square with a slightly lighter Maltese Cross inside it. It was nearly central in the forehead, in approximately the position that Hindus have their oval red spots. The sides of the square were about 1cm. in length, and the impressive thing was that the four right angles at the corners were all very sharp and clearly defined. However, it was not quite a perfect square, because one of the edges was slightly curved. This red mark was obviously made by dilatation of the blood vessels under the surface of the skin, and it faded out over a period of about a week. The lighter Maltese Cross inside the square was the first to go, losing its distinctness so that what remained gave the impression of a simple red square, and this gradually faded.

This subject was well-known to the Institute's staff and the marks on his skin were observed by them immediately on his return from the conference referred to. At first sight it appeared as if the mark had been made deliberately by burning, as the edges were so clear-cut and rectangular. However, on closer inspection it was clear it could not have been produced by this method as there was no raised weal on the skin but merely a red patch.

In a case such as the last quoted, it seems that the mark is produced by a hyperaemia, that is, by an increase in blood flow through the vessels of the skin, causing the skin to appear red. These blood vessels are controlled by the autonomic nervous system, which is not normally subject to conscious control, but is controlled by its own reflexes. Further, the structure of the autonomic nervous system is thought to be relatively diffuse, and to lack the precise control which we associate with our voluntary actions. On the basis of our present physiological knowledge, it is not obvious how an instruction would be given through the nervous system for the blood vessels to dilate according to a pattern on such a small scale, and to create such sharp edges as were actually observed.

★

Another phenomenon which illustrates the increased control of physiological processes which may be possible is the mental control of autonomic functions which, it is alleged, is sometimes shown by Yogis among others. Very few such cases have been adequately investigated, but I shall describe one that apparently was.[1] The chief feature of this experiment was that the subject's oxygen consumption appeared to fall by 40–50% below his basal requirements as a result of the practice of Yogic meditation.

The study in question was made by three Indian physiologists of a subject called Shri Ramanand Yogi of Andhra, who had claimed to have stayed in a sealed underground pit for up to 28 days on previous occasions. The subject was placed in a sealed box, whose oxygen and carbon dioxide content could be measured while he was in it, and from the decline in oxygen and rise in carbon dioxide concentrations in the box his rate of consumption of oxygen could be calculated. This was compared with his 'basal' rate of oxygen consumption, that is, the amount used by a person normally resting and relaxed, and not making any movements.

The consumption of oxygen is of course proportional to the amount of energy being used by the body. The 'basal' rate of oxygen consumption measures approximately the amount of energy being used by a person just to keep ticking over; any reduction in energy consumption below this level indicates a reduction in the degree of activity of physiological functions which are not normally under conscious control; for example, reductions in visceral activity, resting muscle tone, or in thyroid output.

The figures quoted by the authors indicate that while the subject was in the box there was a substantial fall in this resting metabolic activity, to a much lower level than that occurring in sleep, for example.

A remarkable feature of their report is that even after eight hours

[1] B. K. Anand, G. S. Chhina and Baldev Singh, *Indian Journal of Medical Research*, Vol. 49 (1961), pp. 82–9.

in the box, there was no significant increase either in Shri Raman-and's rate of respiration or in his pulse rate. This is despite the fact that by that time the carbon dioxide concentration stood at over 4%.

There is a powerful reflex linking the CO_2 content of the air in the lungs to the rate of respiration, so that normally if one breathes air with a CO_2 content of over 4% it is impossible to avoid breathing very hard indeed, even if one tries not to do so. It seems that Shri Ramanand had been able to over-ride this reflex.

I have quoted this report because it is one of the few attempts to investigate this question of man's control over his own physiology on a scientific basis, not because it is necessarily perfect. For example, the authors do not make clear how they determined 'basal' oxygen consumption for this subject. (I do not mean to imply any acceptance of the social myth that only experimental work on such things as Yogis is less than perfect.)

One might contrast the lack of interest which has been shown in this question, and the almost total absence of experimental investigations to which it is possible to refer, with the continuous stream of experimental findings that are produced concerning, say, the effects of drugs on the nervous system. One may imagine how interested everyone would have been in a drug which was alleged to lower the basal metabolic rate.

*

Even hypnosis has had more of a run for its money than has the study of those phenomena which reveal the possibility that the mind can exercise a much higher degree of control, and possibly conscious control, over physiological functions than is normally the case. This idea is, of course, extremely repellent. Hypnosis was more acceptable because, although it sometimes led to increased control of physiological functions, this was not consciously exercised by the subject, but was exercised only subconsciously and under external direction. It was, in fact, this element of passivity in the hypnotic situation which enabled it to gain social recognition, after a fashion, although few of the potentialities of the hypnotic state are widely known. The notion of the subject as less, and not more, in control of his own mind had an immense appeal, and hypnosis is usually thought of as a means by which a person's mind may be even more than usually subject to external influence.

What is particularly acceptable is the idea of some authoritative agent of the collective, such as a psychotherapist, depriving the individual of his own volition so as to do good to him by influencing him while he is in a state for which he is subsequently amnesic.

CHAPTER 8

The Bonsai Tree

THE Bonsai Tree is a miniature tree created by starvation. If you take the seed of an ordinary tree, such as an oak or an elm, and give it exceedingly little nourishment, it can be made to grow into a minute imitation of a tree of normal size.

This is rather like the treatment which has been accorded to the subject of parapsychology (as it is somewhat invidiously named). Having been most careful to see that the financial resources at the disposal of the subject were minimal, and that the demands made on it were such as could only be met by very large financial resources, the human race has ensured that parapsychology has grown into a wonderfully starved little tree. 'That is a very insignificant species of tree,' everyone says. 'You see how small it grows.'

I described the name parapsychology as invidious, since it at once establishes a position in which the phenomena covered by this label have to struggle for recognition, as something which is not the concern of ordinary psychology or physics. Personally, I do not regard the phenomena in this light. This is why we have called our organisation the Institute of Psychophysical Research. We are interested in all phenomena which bear upon the interaction of the psychological and the physical.

*

It is a fact of human psychology that finding things out is not what it is basically motivated to do. It is motivated to maintain an anthropocentric attitude—to believe that the universe as a whole can spring no surprises on the human race, and to believe that there is something loosely identified with society which has every right totally to possess and evaluate the individual (this thing was formerly called God). Most people's lives are devoted alternately to supporting the social structure, and to receiving support from it. This process is scarcely favourable to the advancement of knowledge.

For example, Freud was convinced that telepathy existed, and remarked that if he had his life again he would like to devote it to research into this and allied phenomena. One may doubt whether in fact he would really have done this in any circumstances, since he was so easily deflected by social considerations from speaking his mind about telepathy. Ernest Jones dissuaded him from any attempt to gain acceptance for the phenomenon of telepathy by pointing out that it was quite difficult enough to gain social respectability for psychoanalysis. However, now that they were beginning to manage quite nicely in this respect, it would be unwise to risk any set-back by championing telepathy as well. As a result, it is scarcely a matter of common knowledge that Freud had any interest at all in telepathy.

It may be supposed that considerations of a similar kind have, consciously or unconsciously, influenced many of those distinguished and even famous men who have taken an interest in these phenomena in the course of the last century. Making loud or urgent noises of any kind is not what society rewards people for doing, still less when the noises concern the importance of research being done in a direction which does not contribute immediately to the idea that society has everything and everybody nicely taped.

Indeed, some of these distinguished people have been known to me, and I have observed their delicacy in, seemingly, not wishing to offend their eminent colleagues by forcing upon their attention any facts which they would prefer not to know concerning unpleasant phenomena. As if by mutual agreement, they have discussed the subject only with others already interested in it. They have published the papers describing their experiments and observations discreetly in a specialised journal of their own, so as to cause no inconvenience by attempting to force them on the attention of the editors of psychological and philosophical journals with a less limited circulation.

The result has been the paradoxical situation which prevails today. Although paranormal phenomena have been studied by a succession of leading academics and intellectuals for a century, no part of the work which has been done has been permitted to become part of the general culture, not even of the general culture of the academic world.

*

A very common belief which many people hold, in the modern implicit manner, is that the way in which the collective human mind works has become completely different in the course of the last few centuries. It is necessary for them to believe this because the dogmatic beliefs which were formerly held by a majority of the people, or by those who dictated what collective opinions should be, are known to have been at variance with things which people believe now. The human race likes to think that it has outgrown 'superstition', so that nowadays it is quite all right, in fact a sign of the utmost rationality and fairmindedness, to take social approval as a guide to what it is correct to believe.

However, what history really demonstrates is this. The human race has an immense capacity for forming dogmatic beliefs and for taking no notice of facts. The human race was once able to believe with great unanimity that the sun went round the earth, and it has been able throughout its recorded history to avoid incorporating in its general culture any distinct information concerning a number of kinds of experience which fairly commonly happen to it, such as out-of-the-body experiences and apparitions.

Curiously enough, the fact that these phenomena are of fairly common occurrence, and it is to be presumed always have been, sometimes seems to be regarded as yet another reason for ignoring them. When we published our books on lucid dreams and out-of-the-body experiences, with the intention of demonstrating that these were distinct classes of phenomena which happened, and which lent themselves readily to further scientific study, particularly under laboratory conditions, a number of psychiatrists and other people wrote to us saying that we need not think we had discovered anything, as such experiences happened very commonly to their patients. Naturally we wrote back saying that we were delighted to hear this, and would be very pleased if they would send us a paper on their observations of these phenomena, so that we could add to the body of knowledge concerning them. This, of course, elicited no reply.

*

There was a medieval belief to the effect that an egg containing a cock chick was more nearly spherical than one which contained a hen chick. It was believed that this was so because the male was more perfect than the female and a sphere was more perfect than an ellipsoid. This has sometimes given rise to amused comment, on the lines of how strange it was that it never occurred to them to measure a few eggs and find out if this were really true. This and similar beliefs are frequently quoted as evidence that the medieval mind was totally different from the enlightened scientific modern one.

On the contrary, one may well think that this proves the medieval mind to have been remarkably similar to the modern one, which also has a remarkable disinterest in finding out anything of a readily ascertainable factual nature which might not produce results quite in conformity with its dogmatic beliefs.

Let us pause for a moment to consider what would have been the likely fate of any peculiar individual who had ventured to produce measurements of a number of actual eggs in support of his disbelief. Is it to be supposed that the protagonists of the spherical egg theory would have been extremely interested? Or that they would have rushed to duplicate these pioneering measurements? On the contrary, they would no doubt have been treated much as any piece of research of a disagreeable nature is treated today— with a superlative display of disinterest. And it is this disinterest, rather than sporadic allegations that the pioneer might have selected an anomalous set of eggs, or made his measurements wrongly, or told lies about the whole thing, which would have eventually frozen him into silence.

It is true that the modern intellectual does not clearly state his dogmatic beliefs, but this renders them the more unassailable. Once you have made a definite assertion that cocks emerge from spherical eggs, your belief is always liable to disproof, provided that there is anyone sufficiently unusual to think of referring to the facts. (Although you may, very properly and cuttingly, ignore him.) If there is a significant difference between a modern mind and the 'unscientific' mind of the past, it is more likely to reside in the greatly improved technique for the protection of dogmatic beliefs by shrouding them in nebulousness. This, naturally, makes it difficult for anyone to oppose them because it is first necessary to state what they are, and you are always liable to be accused of having stated them somewhat wrongly. This must be borne in mind in any attempts which I make to define the essential features of modern dogmatic belief.

However, implicit though these beliefs are, it is interesting to observe that everyone clearly recognises what lines of research are liable to produce results at variance with them. This precise recognition of the situation is manifested by effectively ignoring any development that might tend in the direction of factual information of the wrong kind.

*

The system of belief which was felt to be threatened by the discoveries of Galileo is, in its psychological essentials, remarkably similar to the system of belief which prevails today and which dictates that so many avenues of research should be painstakingly ignored.

The essence of the belief that the sun went round the earth was that it was anthropocentric. Man was supposed to be the most important thing in the universe, and furthermore he had everything absolutely taped in the form of a set of religious beliefs, according to which God also thought that the human race and its various social taboos were of prime importance. This was cosy, self-contained and presented no loose ends.

If modern accepted belief is examined, it is found to come out to much the same thing. The human race is the centre of everything, it has got everything taped in terms of a handful of crude dogmatic beliefs, and it does not want any research to be done which does not immediately contribute to reinforcing its self-confidence. Actually, this rules out rather a lot.

One of the things that the human race has rather an emotional complex about is the idea that there may be higher dimensions of space or time. Presumably this is because the idea of the universe as a mere hyper-surface in a space of perhaps infinitely many dimensions is unacceptable for the same reason that it was unacceptable to think that the earth was not the obvious centre of everything.

At any rate, theoretical physics ran into trouble as soon as it became impossible to avoid noticing how difficult it was to account for the phenomena it was studying in terms of a self-contained three-dimensional space.

In addition to wishing to believe that the only physical universe is safely three-dimensional, the human race also wishes to believe that it knows what is good for everybody. Formerly it was dogmatic religion that provided the prescriptions which had to solve everything. Now it is thought necessary to believe that the human being is a purely physiological entity. This leads to the belief that what is exactly right for everybody can be worked out eventually, even if not quite yet, by the study of biochemistry. That is to say, society will be able to work out what is objectively best for people by reference to observations which do not include consulting the people themselves. Or, to put it another way, it is felt that society can possess and prescribe for the individual with the requisite absoluteness if the individual has no inside—i.e. no consciousness. This accounts for the lack of interest shown in any phenomenon which does suggest that states of consciousness are of any importance, or that there is in any way more to the human mechanism than meets the eye.

And finally, research which in any way invokes the consideration of psychological factors is certain to be done badly. Part of the system of modern beliefs consists of a few crude psychological myths in terms of which all human behaviour must be explained, and which are held to provide an ideal form of psychological adjustment, from which any deviation is to be regarded as 'illness'.[1] Now as this psychological mythology, on which so much sociology, psychiatry and social work is based, disintegrates on analytical consideration, it provides no more favourable environment for any genuine understanding of the psychological factors which may enter into any field of research than did earlier beliefs that people were frequently possessed by evil spirits or that the keeping of sexual taboos was very important as facilitating entrance to heaven after death.

The modern set of dogmatic beliefs which people feel may be upset by the scientific study of the paranormal are not as explicit as the belief in a very literal and dogmatic Christianity which formerly prevailed, but they are equally crude. Implicit though they are, they include a very firm belief that scientific findings must always result in something that can be used to support a very crude kind of materialistic belief. The brain, it is felt, must be something

[1] For a further discussion of this mythology, see my book *The Human Evasion*, Hamish Hamilton, London, 1969.

like a computer, and even if we cannot explain it in any precise way on these terms, we 'ought' to reject or shun any findings which do not immediately appear to make it easier for us to think of the brain in this way. Similarly, the modern dogmatic belief is that certain very crude beliefs about the ideal psychological adjustment of the human being must be correct. The findings of experiment that human beings, under certain circumstances, show signs of faculties, such as those of telepathy and psychokinesis, which are not related to present day psychological theories, immediately suggest that the forms of psychological adjustment, and the personality structures which at present prevail among the human race, may not necessarily be the only ones possible.

*

One thing which has undoubtedly inhibited the progress of research in parapsychology—although perhaps it can hardly be said to inhibit it when sufficient difficulties already exist to render progress virtually non-existent—has been the fact that the human race has a vested interest in being particularly stupid about psychology, and it is impossible to understand much about the psychological factors which enter into the production of paranormal phenomena without permitting oneself to think about psychology more analytically than is usual.

The human race needs to maintain its belief-system about society, including those few myths about psychology which constitute the social stock-in-trade. The psychological notions of Freud have not proved too difficult to assimilate, conveying as they did the image of personality as helplessly conditioned by infantile experiences of interaction with one's family. If Freud's ideas had been difficult to assimilate, they would not have been assimilated, but ignored, as was for instance the work of Myers. However, it cannot be said that the human race has had to do too much ignoring in this department, as it is not common for anyone to show any signs of psychological insight. When they do, their insight is totally misunderstood, and they are accused of being moral monsters, as was the case with Nietzsche and Schopenhauer.

A discussion of the terms on which telepathy and psychokinesis can be done brings us immediately into regions about which people cannot afford to think realistically. For example, a salient feature of many states in which ESP or PK are produced, is the avoidance of individual responsibility, for example by invoking some 'spirit-guide' who is supposed to be the real initiator of the phenomena. Now people's belief in society is intimately bound up with their wish to avoid direct responsibility for knowing their own mind in any way, and it follows that this area of psychology is something they cannot afford to think about in any detail.[1]

Then again, one of the conflicts which has in some way to be avoided or eliminated by the ESP subject is that connected with the feeling that he is in some way on trial, and that people are expecting him to prove he can do ESP. Now the image of the individual as being on trial by society is very strong in human psychology, as indeed the attitudes to parapsychology discussed in this book will partially demonstrate, and people cannot afford to think in an objective way about the implications of this scenario, and the damaging effect which it may be having, not only on people's ability to do ESP, but on their ability to function efficiently in other areas as well.

*

Orthodox science likes to give the impression that the phenomena which it ignores, under the general heading of the 'paranormal', are in any event an extremely small and insignificant field of study. However, the size of the field of study which science is choosing to ignore cannot be measured by the amount of attention which is bestowed on it. It cannot be at all safely assumed that, even if telepathy is ever admitted to respectability, it will only be as a tiny fringe area of psychology proper, of interest only to specialists. Nor can it be assumed that if lucid dreams are ever examined with the thoroughness they deserve, they will emerge as a tiny and specialised sub-division of the study of dreams. On the contrary, it may well appear in the future that those areas of investigation which modern science chooses to consider scientific, because they offer support to the prevailing world-view, constitute a very small selection from the field of phenomena which should properly be the concern of scientific research.

[1] For a discussion of the topic of responsibility in relation to ESP and PK see Charles McCreery, *Science, Philosophy and ESP*, in particular Chapter IX ('Dissociated *versus* Conscious ESP').

CHAPTER 9

Extrasensory Perception

IT has been pointed out that it is quite possible to go on believing in any outmoded scientific theory, provided you are prepared to elaborate it sufficiently to accommodate subsequent findings. For example, it would be quite possible to devise a complicated version of the phlogiston theory to conform to modern chemical knowledge. This is merely a form of the total uncertainty, as a result of which it is impossible to prove anything absolutely. If people were realistic, they would bear this uncertainty in mind even in connection with those beliefs which give them the greatest sense of security, such as their belief that the sun will rise tomorrow, and that feeding the starving millions is a good thing. As a matter of fact, of course, they do not bear in mind that even such assertions are strictly unprovable, but they make use of the total uncertainty when shrugging off the evidence for extrasensory perception and other paranormal phenomena.

Those with an interest in parapsychology tend to demonstrate their social conscience by pretending that there is something about the study of paranormal phenomena which is quite exceptionally difficult, and in particular they complain that extrasensory perception does not happen to everybody, all of the time, at will. But in fact no scientific phenomenon can be said to have yielded repeatable experiments until the conditions appropriate to observing it had been understood. One might just as well complain that astronomical observations were not 'repeatable' because they could not be made at any time with the naked eye.

And, as a matter of fact, it is not necessary to 'believe' that telepathy is absolutely proven in order to consider that phenomena are present which should be investigated. But this is a decision which has to be made by individuals. Looking back on the

scientists of the past, not many of them would have got far if they
had sought the collective approval of mankind before carrying out
their investigations.

It is an absurdity not to think that the evidence warrants investigation of the paranormal, but the human race is evidently
capable of such absurdities.

It was thirty years after Semmelweis pointed out the manifest
desirability of doctors disinfecting their hands before attending
women in child-birth that the human race finally accepted the idea.
And then, of course, it was not as a result of the efforts of Semmelweis, whom they had driven to end his life in an asylum.

Incidentally, it is very curious that even people who accept the
evidence for telepathy and so forth have a psychological need to
believe that it is very difficult to make progress in this field, instead of accepting what is in fact the case, that only being syste-
matically starved of money can prevent the subject from making
certain very important advances by developing in various perfectly
obvious directions.

Evidence for extrasensory perception occurs, at times, in any of
a wide variety of states. Evidence of high calibre has been reported
with subjects in the waking state, in ordinary dreams, in lucid
dreams, in out-of-the-body experiences, in various trance states,
and under the influence of hypnosis. We shall proceed to illustrate some of these possibilities. It should be realised that the
examples given are not necessarily the most strikingly evidential
ones that could be given, but are intended to illustrate the possible
operation of ESP in the various states in question.[1]

The following account by Oliver Fox concerns two examples of
lucid dreams which suggest the possible operation of ESP.

> Two isolated experiments may be noted here:
> On the eve of sitting for an examination in machine construction,
> I willed to dream of seeing the paper that would be set. I dreamed
> that I was taking the examination, and, knowing that I was dream-
> ing, attempted to memorize the questions upon the paper. On
> awakening, I remembered two: (1) Sketch and describe some form
> of steam-separator. (2) Sketch a grease-box suitable for a goods-
> truck. The next day, when I actually took the examination, I found

[1] For a discussion of some evidence for ESP, see *Science, Philosophy
and ESP* (Hamish Hamilton, 1972) by my colleague Charles McCreery,
Chapters 1–3.

both these questions upon the paper. They did not appear as complete questions by themselves, but were sections of others. The first was a likely question; but a perusal of past papers (made *after* the dream) showed that the second question had not been asked for many years.

. . . The other experiment was as follows:

I had been spending the evening with two friends, Slade and Elkington, and our conversation had turned to the subject of dreams. Before parting, we agreed to meet, if possible, on Southampton Common in our dreams that night. I dreamed I met Elkington on the Common as arranged, but Slade was not present. We both knew we were dreaming and commented on Slade's absence. After which the dream ended, being of very short duration. The next day when I saw Elkington I said nothing at first of my experience, but asked him if he had dreamed. 'Yes,' he replied, 'I met you on the Common all right and knew I was dreaming, but old Slade didn't turn up. We had just time to greet each other and comment on his absence, then the dream ended.' On interviewing Slade we learned that he had not dreamed at all, which perhaps accounted for his inability to keep the appointment.

Some people have raised the objection, 'Oh, well, you expected to meet your friend and so you dreamed you did. That's all.' But if expectation is to explain the experience, then I expected to meet Elkington and *Slade*, while Elkington expected to meet *Slade* and me. How is it, then, expectation failed us both with regard to Slade ? Why was he absent ? How is it expectation failed to make him dream of meeting us ? Elkington and I were unable to repeat this small success. (Oliver Fox, *Astral Projection*, University Books, New York, 1962, pp. 45–7.)

The following is an example of a 'waking dream' which suggests the possible operation of ESP. The percipient, Mr. Field, is a Chartered Accountant:

24th September, 1966

I have had a great number of experiences of telepathy but the strangest occurrence took place on a Sunday afternoon early in January 1947.

I was reading a newspaper at home here, when suddenly I realized that I was standing in Fore Street, Totnes (13 miles away) and I saw that Mr. N. K. V. Clarke, the Manager of my Branch Office there, was walking down the passage leading to it.

I told my late wife what I had seen and on her expressing incredulity, I dialed the Totnes telephone number and I remember that I was not at all surprised when the telephone was answered by Mr. N. K. V. Clarke.

Mr. Clarke remembers the incident as follows:

17th January, 1967

I well remember the incident. At the time I was a Manager of Mr. Field's Totnes Branch of his Accountancy Practice, and I lived in a flat in Totnes, and Mr. Field lived some 13 miles away in Kingsbridge.

On the Sunday afternoon in question it was raining, and my wife was busy with house-work in our small flat, and I had a considerable amount of work to do in the office, and I decided to go into the office to do two hours work. So far as I can recollect I arrived at 3 o'clock, and I had just started work when the telephone bell rang. I nearly jumped out of my skin, for I hardly expected a telephone call, and nobody except my wife knew that I was in the office. Our flat was not on the telephone, so there is no method by which she could have told anybody that they could find me in the office.

I remember picking up the telephone and Mr. Field said 'Good afternoon Mr. Clarke', and recognising his voice I said 'Hello, how the devil did you know that I was in the office this afternoon?' and he replied that he had seen me walking into the office only a few minutes beforehand, which was correct.

So far as he was concerned he could have had no prior knowledge that I intended to go into the office, indeed, until after lunch I had no intention of doing so.

This is not the only occasion when incidents such as this have arisen, but it is the only occasion for which there seems to be no material reason for Mr. Field's knowing that I was in the office. The other numerous incidents which arose during our professional connection could be traced to some material fact, albeit somewhat remote at times.

In this last instance the extrasensory information, if such it was, was incorporated in a complete hallucinatory environment which temporarily replaced the percipient's real environment. In other cases people report experiencing inexplicable and often compelling urges to do things, without any hallucinatory accompaniment. The following is a rather characteristic example of apparent telepathy in the waking state (or conceivably during the sleeping state immediately preceding it) resulting in a strong impulse, in this case to go and visit a relative.

September, 1966

Five years ago I sat reading the paper one afternoon and must have fallen asleep. The next thing I remember was waking very suddenly, and seeing the clock showing 2.45 p.m. I put on a coat and caught the 2.50 p.m. bus to my niece's house.

When I was walking along the road to her house I couldn't think why on earth I was going to visit her, as it was Tuesday and I *always* regularly visited her Wednesday. When I opened the door, she came out of the dining room and said, 'Oh, Auntie Anne, I have been wanting you to come; Martin (her son aged six) has been taken suddenly ill and I am waiting for the doctor to come.' Little Martin died during the night. I didn't have any way of knowing he was ill; so what made me go? (I had helped to rear my niece; we are very close.)

The subject's niece remembers the incident as follows:

18.10.66

This is to verify that my aunt, Mrs. M., came to my house one Tuesday when my little boy was taken ill. An illness from which he died a few hours later.

Her visit was unexpected as, for a very long time, she had visited regularly on Wednesdays.

The following case will illustrate the possible operation of ESP under hypnosis. The subject was a woman called Jane, the wife of a Durham pitman. According to F. W. H. Myers, who collected the evidence, the lady in question 'most carefully concealed her faculty from all her neighbours and relations, except her husband and sister, for fear of being taken for a witch.' Myers introduces one particular instance of her phenomena as follows:

She was hypnotised at intervals for many years from 1845 onwards, for the sake of her health, and used then to ask to 'travel'—that is, to be guided by suggestion to places which she should clairvoyantly visit. The main evidence about her is contained in the contemporaneous notes of a Dr. F., which, however, do not appear to have been made before the truth of her statements was verified. I quote an extract from these notes.

Before commencing the sitting I fixed to take her to a house, without communicating my intentions to any of the parties present. In the morning of the day I stated to a patient of my own, Mr. Eglinton, at present residing in the village of Tynemouth, that I intended to visit him. He stated that he would be present between 8 and 10 P.M. in a particular room, so that there might be no difficulty in finding him. He was just recovering from a very severe illness, and was so weak that he could scarcely walk. He was exceedingly thin from the effects of his complaint.

After the usual state had been obtained, I said, 'We are standing beside a railway station, now we pass along a road, and in front of us see a house with a laburnum tree in front of it.' She directly replied, 'Is it the red house with a brass knocker?' I said, 'No, it has an iron knocker.' I have since looked, however, and find that the door has an old-fashioned brass handle in the shape of a knocker. She then asked,

'Shall we go up the steps ? Shall we go along this passage and up these
stairs ? Is this a window on the stair head ?' I said, 'You are quite
right, and now I want you to look into the room upon the left-hand
side.' She replied, 'Oh yes, in the bedroom. There is no one in this
room; there is a bed in it, but there is no person in it.' I was not
aware that a bedroom was in the place I mentioned, but upon inquiry next day I found she was correct. I told her she must look into
the next room and she would see a sofa. She answered, 'But there is
here a little gallery. Now I am in the room, and see a lady with black
hair lying upon the sofa.' I attempted to puzzle her about the colour
of her hair, and feeling sure it was Mr. Eglinton who was lying there,
I sharply cross-questioned her, but still she persisted in her story. The
questioning, however, seemed to distract her mind, and she commenced talking about a lady at Whickham, until I at last recalled her
to the room at Tynemouth by asking her whether there was not a
gentleman in the room. 'No,' she said; 'we can see no gentleman
there.'

After a little she described the door opening, and asked with a
tone of great surprise, 'Is that a gentleman ?' I replied, 'Yes; is he
thin or fat ?' 'Very fat,' she answered; 'but has he a cork leg ?' I
assured her that he had no cork leg, and tried to puzzle her again
about him. She, however, assured me that he was very fat and had a
great corporation, and asked me whether I did not think such a fat
man must eat and drink a great deal to get such a corporation as that.
She also described him as sitting by the table with papers beside him,
and a glass of brandy and water. 'Is it not wine ?' I asked. 'No,' she
said, 'it's brandy.' 'Is it not whisky or rum ?' 'No, it is brandy,' was
the answer; 'and now,' she continued, 'the lady is going to get her
supper, but the fat gentleman does not take any.' I requested her to
tell me the colour of his hair, but she only answered that the lady's
hair was dark. I then inquired if he had any brains in his head, but
she seemed altogether puzzled about him, and said she could not see
any. I then asked her if she could see his name upon any of the
letters lying about. She replied, 'Yes;' and upon my saying that the
name began with E, she spelt each letter of the name 'Eglinton'.

I was so convinced that I had at last detected her in a complete
mistake that I arose, and declined proceeding further in the matter,
stating that, although her description of the house and the name of
the person were correct, in everything connected with the gentleman
she had guessed the opposite from the truth.

On the following morning Mr. E. asked me the result of the experiment, and after having related it to him, he gave me the following
account: He had found himself unable to sit up to so late an hour,
but wishful fairly to test the powers of the clairvoyante, he had ordered
his clothes to be stuffed into the form of a figure, and to make the
contrast more striking to his natural appearance, had an extra pillow
pushed into the clothes so as to form a 'corporation'. This figure had
been placed near the table, in a sitting position, and a glass of brandy

and water and the newspapers placed beside it. The name, he further added, was spelt correctly, though up to that time I had been in the habit of writing it 'Eglington', instead of as spelt by the clair-voyante, 'Eglinton'. (F. W. H. Myers, *Human Personality*, Vol. I, pp. 553-4.)

No absolutely simple way exists at present of making ESP mani-fest itself continuously in any one of the states in which it sometimes happens. Each of the states is habitually regarded, not as an object of investigation in its own right, but as a method for obtaining evidence that ESP exists. There appears to lurk in the minds of parapsychologists a curious persuasion that extrasensory percep-tion may one day become continuously and consistently available in some one of these states, without their having to get to know anything about how it works. It is felt that to do this would be anti-social or unsporting. It is rather as if the first astronomers had decided that it would be taking an unfair advantage to construct a telescope, and perhaps one day the laws of optics might conveni-ently change so that astronomical observations of the required accuracy could be made without one.

Thus, on hearing that a certain hypnotist has a certain subject who happens to be able to do successful ESP, what occurs to the mind of the socially-adjusted parapsychologist is not bringing to bear on the situation the resources of modern neuro-physiology (such as they are) so that we may at least discover as accurately as possible whether, and in what ways, this subject's state when he is doing successful ESP differs from his state when he is trying to do ESP but not being particularly successful, and also from his nor-mal unhypnotised state. No indeed! What occurs to the para-psychological mind is to get another hypnotist to hypnotise another subject to see whether he too can produce some more evidence for ESP, apparently in the expectation that the first hypnotist's success has signalised a radical change in the state of affairs. It is no longer (perhaps) the case that ESP occurs sporadi-cally, with certain subjects, for reasons which no one understands or has made any attempt to study, in a wide variety of states of which hypnosis is one. No, it is possible that ESP has suddenly decided to make itself freely available in the hypnotic state, so we had better test this hypothesis by doing some more hypnosis. It might, of course, be held to demonstrate an unwonted awareness of the total uncertainty that so improbable and imaginative a hypothesis should be entertained and actually acted upon. However, I must admit this hypothesis is not exactly what would first spring to my own mind.

Similarly, if some subject were to produce evidential ESP with his twin brother acting as agent, there would doubtless break out a rash of attempts (albeit half-hearted ones) to obtain further evidence for the existence of ESP by experimenting with pairs of twins.

There are not a few people who consider that their eminence in other fields renders them particularly suitable to be the person who will make the Great Break-Through in parapsychology. Their thoughts habitually work upon inventing some ingenious combination of circumstances in which, it may be, ESP will consent to operate with the required freedom and consistency. ESP has not hitherto manifested itself to order, but perhaps it will be found to do so if we have seven agents to every two percipients and hang dark red curtains between them. Psychokinesis has not previously been produced to order by all subjects in the hypnotic state; maybe the necessary condition to make it do so is that the subjects should be seated in jockey chairs, which will register the slightest diminution of their weight.

It follows that a great many of the experiments cannot, even if successful, do more than add to the evidence that ESP exists. None of them has yet succeeded in hitting upon a magical combination of external circumstances which will make extrasensory perception show itself to order, without our having to take the trouble to understand it.

Incidentally, the way in which electrophysiological apparatus is used seems to provide additional evidence of a curious mental bias on the part of the experimenters. One might suppose that the obvious function of such apparatus would be to examine variations in the condition of a given subject, and to seek for ways of differentiating between his condition in periods of successful ESP, and his condition at other times. However, what we find is that electrophysiological apparatus is being used to provide evidence for ESP. For example, if both subject and percipient are connected to a plethysmograph (which measures the blood-flow through a finger), and if their two sets of plethysmographic readings show a significant degree of agreement, this is held to demonstrate that they have communicated their emotional states to one another by telepathy.

It is difficult to think of any other field in which the concepts of 'proving' and 'finding out about' something have been divorced in the way they are in connection with the paranormal.

When people began to be aware of electricity, they did not spend all their time arguing about whether their initial experiments had been mistaken or fraudulent or misreported. They went ahead and did more experiments, and by the time a good deal was known about the way electricity worked, it had become rather absurd for anyone to say they did not regard it as 'proved'.

In dealing with telepathy or psychokinesis, there is a great tendency for everyone to suppose that what must be done is to 'prove' to the satisfaction of everyone in the world that it exists, without venturing to try to find out how it works. Suggestions for finding out more about it are liable to be treated as unscientific, because they are supposed to imply a 'belief' in it.

Parapsychologists, therefore, to the extent that they try to do anything, set up more and more experiments the interest of which depends entirely on whether or not they provide additional evidence that telepathy or psychokinesis exist. Such experiments are in the nature of things unsatisfactory. What happens, time and again, is that a series of experiments does provide evidence for the existence of telepathy, is ignored by the scientific world at large, and begins to fade into the past, which makes it even easier to ignore it, and some considerable time after the end of the experiment—say, twenty or thirty years, but at any rate too late for anything definite to be established one way or the other—someone starts to suggest some ingenious method by which everyone concerned in the experiments might have been cheating.

This will of course continue to be the case so long as experiments are designed to provide evidence and nothing else.

The obsession with the evidential has led to many obvious ways in which knowledge could have been advanced being ignored. For example, investigators were only interested in those out-of-the-body experiences in which the subject saw events at a distance from his physical body, and in which corroboration of the correctness of his paranormally obtained information could be obtained from other people present at the time. This meant that the only interest which could be seen in out-of-the-body experiences was that they were yet another means for providing proof of telepathy.

The following is a case of the evidential kind which interested investigators:

In June 1884 I had been suffering with an ear trouble and had become deaf in my right ear and suffered intensely. At Bradford, Pennsylvania, I consulted with Dr. C. H. Reid and was advised to submit to an operation. I made arrangements to have him come to my house and perform the operation. He came with an assistant and they delivered gas. They told me what to do in inhaling, but told me nothing of how the operation would be performed. They placed me on a lounge with a spread over it and at the head of the lounge had a stand for the instruments. I lay on my back with my hands clasped and began breathing in the gas.

The sensation was pleasant and it seemed as if I was listening to pleasant music. Suddenly I realized I was becoming unconscious. I thought that I did not care to take too much of it and that I would make the doctors think I was unconscious so I let my hands gradually slip apart and just as my finger tips separated I felt as if I raised up from the couch and found myself standing in the corner of the room and rubbing my eyes and feeling very sleepy. I stood facing the wall but turned around and could not think what was going on. There were the two doctors and someone lying on the couch and all at once it occurred to me that the person on the couch was myself and that I was going to see the operation. I heard Dr. Reid say, 'There—he has enough, turn him over and be careful of the pillow, don't smother him,' and it amused me. I went around on the back side of the couch to see the operation and saw the doctor take a knife from his case on the stand and the assistant place a towel to catch the blood. In the operation I saw a small artery cut and the blood spurted so that I jumped out of the way. One doctor caught it with a pair of nippers and the other fastened it. In the operation I saw the doctor take another knife from the case and get a spot of blood on some buckskin it was wrapped in which I afterwards told him of.

After the operation I saw them cleanse the cut with a syringe, unroll a paper on the stand, take out some substance and with an instrument begin to put this into the wound. I tried to remonstrate with them thinking it would dry in, but they paid no attention to me and I became much enraged. It finally occurred to me that they did not know I was there and I must see things away from where my body was lying or they would not believe I saw the operation. Finally they finished dressing the cut and Dr. Reid told his assistant to take away the towels so I would not see the blood and I laughed heartily. He rolled up the towels and took them out into the hall and stuck them under a stand. I saw the letter 'S' on the towels as they were lying there. I went back into the room ahead of the doctor and Dr. Reid was laying aside his instruments. His assistant felt my wrist and said, 'I don't feel any pulse.' They turned the body over. Dr. Reid reached over to the stand for some restorative and I went back into my body as easily as putting on a coat and sat up just as he was uncorking the bottle. I made them look up the towels to see that I had described them correctly and also examine the blood spot on the buckskin and I then described the operation and told them all they did and said. (*Proceedings of the S.P.R.*, Vol. 53, 1962, pp. 288–289.)

This account was accompanied by a letter of corroboration from Dr. Reed (the correct spelling), confirming the fact that events had taken place during the operation as the patient had described them.

In fact, of course, only a small proportion of all the ecsomatic cases which occur do provide high-grade evidence for ESP, complete with corroboration of this kind. Out-of-the-body experiences as a phenomenon which happens fairly commonly to quite a large percentage of human beings, and which is in itself at variance with existing suppositions concerning sensory perception, were totally ignored.

When this Institute made an appeal for out-of-the-body cases in 1966 there was no prior work to give any indication of what the response was likely to be. In fact it rapidly became apparent that these experiences happened quite commonly, and we were able to make a detailed study of their characteristics, the results of which were published in my book *Out-of-the-Body Experiences* (Hamish Hamilton, 1968). This was the first study of the characteristics of out-of-the-body experiences considered as a phenomenon in their own right. This study, interesting though it was, now needs to be carried further by observations which can only be made in an electrophysiological laboratory and this we will do as soon as we have the necessary funds.

*

There is in human psychology a very dominant image. This is the image of the individual 'proving himself' or 'justifying' what he wants to do to society before being allowed to proceed. Everyone is taught from an early age that they should regard other people's opinions of them as more important than their own opinions of themselves. And in adult life people tend to live, in a very implicit way, in accordance with this image.

This, needless to say, is extremely inhibiting to the progress of any research which does not immediately support current belief. The great supposition is that the opinion of society in its collective manifestations is particularly objective, and that it is up to the individual who wishes to pursue novel lines of research to gain the objective stamp of collective approval before proceeding. As a matter of fact, of course, collective social approval is, as it always has been, very firmly based on the current set of anthropocentric beliefs, and it is no more inclined to objectivity and open-minded-ness now than it was when it imprisoned Galileo. However, those who take some interest in extrasensory perception are exceedingly inclined to behave as if their first objective had to be to convince society at large, and not themselves, that these researches should be pursued, which is rather as though Galileo had set out to prove to the Inquisition that looking through a telescope was a worth-while activity before he allowed himself to notice anything which he saw when he looked through it. So the theme tune of such research as there has been on extrasensory perception has been the attempt to obtain, on extremely restricted terms, evidence of the kind which the world might be supposed to appreciate that extrasensory perception existed at all. This has been combined with a striking lack of attention to the conditions in which ESP occurred, as though it would only be proper to take notice of such factors when society had given its approval to such research.

Along with the image of objective collectivity passing judge-ment on individuals, there goes a kind of belief that it should be possible to convince these forces of the collective that something is worth doing very *cheaply*. Until you have gained the support of society at large, you should not think of doing anything that would cost much money anyway. This not only fits with the idea that pioneering work can (for some curious and unstated reason) always be done without money, but also fits with the idea of the maso-chistic attitude which anyone is supposed to have who does some-thing before society has given its blessing. Such pioneers are supposed to want to work in the most cramped and constricted conditions, taking ten years over a project which need take only one if properly financed. It is taken for granted that they should wish to come as near as possible to ruining their health, boring themselves to death by doing everything in the slowest and most arduous way. This attitude has, of course, to be combined with a total direction of their attention, not towards finding anything out about what they are investigating, but towards supplicating the acceptance of society for the existence of extrasensory perception, which they should wish to prove only in those ways which will give society the most favourable opportunity for remaining unimpressed.

However, there are a number of things wrong with the cheapness hypothesis. One of them is that the only forms of research which can be done cheaply are those which orthodox science has shown itself most capable of shrugging off. Indeed, it is virtually declared as a principle that work of this kind can be ignored. For example, if one makes a study of cases of lucid dreams, a great deal may in fact emerge about the characteristics of lucid dreams, which establishes them as a quite distinct state of consciousness in their own right, following quite different intellectual and emotional laws from non-lucid dreams. Certainly this particular information could not be derived in any way but by the study of case material. However, we know that psychologists will find it easy to ignore this work because it was not carried out in an electrophysiological laboratory.

Now I do not myself think that the study of reports of experiences should be ignored in this way. However, certain things could be discovered about lucid dreams in an electrophysiological laboratory which cannot be discovered merely by a study of case material, and the psychologists would have one less line of defence in ignoring the findings that would result from such work. I do not mean to say that orthodox psychologists can ever be forced to take notice of the phenomena of lucid dreams and out-of-the-body experiences, because it is impossible to put into people motivation which is not there. But since they have an established principle that work which is done with certain kinds of apparatus is to be regarded as objective and scientific, while any work that is done by studying subjects' reports is not scientific and objective, they could plainly be made more uncomfortable if one were to produce a continuous supply of out-of-the-body experiences as measured with such apparatus. This, however, can only be done if one has an electrophysiological laboratory, and sufficient staff to run it. This is expensive.

What we have just said is, in fact, only one example of something that is generally true. The types of work in parapsychology which would have the most impact on the scientific world are all expensive, because the scientific world in this century has decided that only certain types of work, which have the incidental characteristic of being very expensive, are scientific. As the subject of parapsychology is totally starved of money (at any rate in the hands of anyone who wishes to use it effectively), this is obviously something of an impasse. As indeed, perhaps it is meant to be.

When we did a mass experiment on ESP and made a birth-order prediction which was fulfilled,[1] various psychologists of my acquaintance said they were certainly very surprised that we had got a statistically significant result. Then they added, brightly, 'Why don't you do it again?' Doing it once had strained our resources to the uttermost, quite apart from various other practical considerations which made it impossible for us to do it again. In any case, they did not say what their reaction would be if we did succeed in repeating it and obtaining an equally significant result. They did not say that they would then assist us in obtaining finance to undertake a more extensive programme of research. In fact, I could only imagine that in such an eventuality their reaction would again be 'Well I *am* surprised! Why don't you do it again?'

This reaction is curiously universal. Once, thinking that I understood how the psychology of ESP worked, I tried to put myself into the state of mind that I thought should be favourable, and scored 13, 9, 7, 10 and 15 on five separate runs of Zener cards. I gave these figures to a young statistician with whom I happened to be working at the time, and he calculated the odds against these being due to chance as greater than a thousand million to one. He said, very seriously, 'You should repeat the experiment.' In fact, I made no attempt to do so. My initial interest in seeing whether I could work out for myself how to do ESP had passed, and the circumstances of my life were too grim and gruelling to make readily accessible the type of detached elation which I found favourable. I had achieved these scores by attempting to guess a pack of Zener cards only when I felt myself to be in a favourable state. To continue making attempts when I did not feel myself to be in such a state would not have been repeating the experiment at all.

This example illustrates the total lack of consideration of psychological problems (which usually reduce to financial ones) which is shown not only by orthodox scientists who have no knowledge of the subject and do not wish to have, but also by people who have made a study of earlier research.

[1] C. E. Green, M. E. Eastman, and S. T. Adams, 'Birth Order, Family Size and Extrasensory Perception', *British Journal of Social and Clinical Psychology*, Vol. V, 1966, pp. 150–2.

Among such people it is more or less universally agreed that a person's emotional state at the time of attempting ESP has a highly significant bearing on their success. This, perhaps curiously, is a matter of more universal agreement than whether there is sufficient evidence to prove the existence of ESP. It is also recognised that the personality and outlook of the agent as well as the percipient and also of any experimenters involved, may be found to affect the outcome. In certain statistical experiments it has been shown that different experimenters obtained significantly different results, all other conditions being equal. Various reports of spontaneous phenomena also support the importance of the agent's psychology.

It is not difficult to find people who expatiate most freely on the deeply emotional nature of telepathy, and the need for subjects to be in surroundings which permit them to feel warm and human and uplifted. However, these same people often demonstrate the most Scrooge-like attitudes towards those hapless persons who wish to do research in the subject. Pioneers ought to want to demonstrate their dedication by living in penury, and by attempting experiments in circumstances so miserable and constricted that they would be doomed to failure from the outset, and on about one per cent of the finance which any research worker in a socially approved field would expect to have before attempting to carry out an experiment of that type.

Of course, this disregard for the well-being, indeed for the bare health and vitality, of those doing pioneering research owes something to the agreeable tradition of geniuses having a thoroughly romantic time starving in garrets. It is probably reinforced, in modern times, by the attempt to eliminate thinking from all fields of human activity, and certainly from research where it is liable to have particularly unpredictable consequences. It is perhaps not surprising that this should lead to a disregard for the conditions actually necessary to enable any intellectual or imaginative process to take place. One feels that the ideal kind of research, even in socially approved fields of science, would be one in which the experiments could be carried out by a tired spastic of low I.Q., operating suitably elaborate machinery in a fog.

*

As we have observed, there is more agreement among parapsychologists concerning the influence of emotional states on ESP, than about whether there is such a thing as ESP. This illustrates the desirability of studying the conditions under which the phenomena occur.

It has, in fact, been pointed out that, since even the most successful subjects at the present time are not uniformly successful, the significance of ESP experiments could be immeasurably enhanced if they were able to identify correctly their successful scoring sessions, or even individual correct guesses, by reference to their introspective observations. If the subject were able to indicate which of his guessing sequences he thought had been successful, and if he were right a high proportion of the time, unsuccessful sessions could be rejected from the analysis (of course before the experimenter or anyone else knew the actual score). And if only high-scoring ESP sessions were included, and others rejected, our experiments with any given subject might be called repeatable. This approach should certainly be attempted, by anyone possessing enough initiative and psychological insight to train their subjects in assessing their internal states, although it has certain draw-backs to which I shall return later.

A far better approach would be to measure various electrophysiological variables and use these to discriminate between a subject's successful ESP states, and the circumstances in which he is not likely to be successful. This could not only be used with successful subjects, but might well enable us to predict with *any* subject whether he was in an appropriate state to do successful ESP, and at the same time enable us to find out something objective about the physiological conditions of ESP.[1] All that is needed for such work to proceed, and to make a highly significant contribution to science, is a well-equipped electrophysiological laboratory, specially designed to accommodate ESP subjects, together with sufficient money to run it and employ the necessary ancillary staff, under the direction of someone who is motivated to use it to find something out.

I do not actually think that the motivation to find things out is very common, and I cannot think of anyone apart from myself and

---

[1] This approach has been fully outlined by my colleague Charles McCreery in his book *Science, Philosophy and ESP*, Chapters 8–13.

my colleagues at the Institute whom I could recommend to carry out such work.

There are, as I have already said, certain draw-backs in training ESP subjects to recognise their successful ESP states without at the same time making use of electrophysiological measurements. For one thing, the information gained will not be readily communicable from one subject to another, since the introspective criteria which have to be used are extremely refined, and people are not in the habit of discussing what they observe going on inside themselves in an extremely analytical way. Then, even if one subject, or even several subjects, learn to recognise introspectively when they are doing ESP, we are scarcely any nearer making generalisations about the conditions which favour ESP. A person of a suitable degree of introspective skill and psychological insight might, it is true, form an idea what the common factors were in the favourable states of mind described by subjects.

As a matter of fact, I do not know anyone whom I could recommend as having the psychological insight necessary to do this apart from myself. As previously mentioned, I have actually worked out to my own satisfaction the psychological conditions necessary for the production of ESP, and if circumstances were favourable I would train the present staff of the Institute to do it. However, this is out of the question while our lives are conducted in such straitened circumstances.

In any case, an introspective understanding of the conditions favourable to ESP would have no power to impress the scientific world, nor would it offer much hope, until interpreted into some other form, of leading on to further lines of research relating ESP to other branches of science.

You have only to consider how different the attitude of the scientific world would be to the statement that successful ESP subjects had in common a particular kind of detachment, and something like expectancy, which could not be exactly described in current psychological vocabulary, and the statement that successful ESP subjects have in common an alpha-rhythm which is accelerated above their normal average. The latter has the characteristics of an objective scientific statement, of a kind which scientists pretend they would not ignore, but it is obviously a much more expensive type of proposition to investigate.

Incidentally, we have already made this prediction on the basis of our studies of the literature—that, in fact, the alpha-rhythm of successful subjects would be found to be accelerated above their normal average. This was eventually confirmed, apparently without any deliberate intention of testing this hypothesis, in some experiments at the University of Virginia, U.S.A., carried out by Rex Stanford and others.[1] It should be pointed out that this was not intended to be the only, or the best, prediction of the kind which someone with adequate facilities would soon be able to make. On the contrary it seemed to us a prediction so crude that it was possible to make it on the basis of other people's published work, without facilities of our own. In fact, I consider that, to be successful, the electrophysiological characteristics of the ESP state should be studied, not crudely, but in as subtle and complicated a way as possible. In making this prediction we were attempting to demonstrate that if we could make any bricks at all without straw, we should be able to make much better bricks if we had some.

Now this sort of experiment, if done in a determined and efficient manner, could eventually make the position of the scientific world in ignoring ESP look distinctly peculiar (at any rate to those who did not kindly avert their gaze) and presumably for this reason it is virtually impossible to get anyone to understand it. I shall be referring later to the concept of invincible stupidity. It is, of course, impossible to demonstrate by force of logic that any two ideas must necessarily be seen as associated. Suppose someone were to say in a puzzled fashion, 'It is very interesting what you say about two and two, but why should it have anything to do with four?' in the same way that they say, 'Lucid dreams are very fascinating, but what have they to do with science?', or, 'What you say about electrophysiology is very interesting, but how could it have anything to do with ESP?' You will, if you are willing, perceive that it would be quite impossible to convince

[1] I first made this prediction in my B.Litt. Thesis 'An Inquiry into some States of Consciousness and their Physiological Foundation, with Special Reference to those in which Extrasensory Perception is Reported to Occur', Oxford, 1960, and my colleague Charles McCreery repeated it in his book *Science, Philosophy and ESP*, first published in 1967. For an account of the experiments by Stanford see Charles McCreery, *Psychical Phenomena and the Physical World*, Hamish Hamilton, 1973, Chapter 10.

them, if whatever one said they continued to repeat, 'But what has that got to do with it?'

I have great experience in the variety of human reactions that are produced when one expounds this virtually cast-iron method for advancing knowledge of ESP—in fact, for forcibly changing its status altogether. The responses provoked show evidence of a wide variety of thought-disorders. For example, it is virtually impossible to get anyone to remember for more than a sentence at a time that it would be necessary to relate a subject's electrophysiological readings when doing ESP to his *own average state*, and not to the average for the population as a whole, or even to his own average for the period immediately before the ESP test as was done in Stanford's experiments. This means that the experiments would have to be much more elaborate, leisurely and therefore expensive than experiments in this subject are usually allowed to be.

It is even more difficult to convince people that what one is talking about is taking measurements in order to study what the electrophysiological conditions are which accompany ESP, and that one is not talking about making use of an EEG to train subjects to recognise when various rhythms are present, or using the EEG to detect parallelisms between the brain rhythms of agent and percipient which would provide evidence for the existence of ESP.

CHAPTER 10

Metachoric Experiences in General

THERE are three classes of hallucinatory experiences which, if studied, would remind people of the mind's capacity for the construction of hallucinatory environments, and hence of the philosophical possibility that the whole of normal perception may be illusory. These are lucid dreams, out-of-the-body experiences and apparitions.

A lucid dream is a dream in which the dreamer is aware that he is dreaming. The following are two examples reported by the nineteenth-century French marquis, Hervey de Saint-Denys, in which he experiments with volition in lucid dreams:

> I dreamt that I was in a garden walk. I was aware that I was dreaming, and thought of the various problems which I was interested in studying. There was a branch of flowering lilac in front of me. I considered it with genuine attention. I remembered having read that memories of smell are rarely accurate in dreams. I took hold of the branch, and assured myself that the smell of the lilac was indeed summoned up by its association with the related impressions connected with the imaginary, but *voluntary*, act. Now, I said to myself, what I am perceiving is an image of an intact, oblong head of lilac of a particular shape, still connected to its bush. Is this a stereotyped image, the unvarying reproduction of some memory-image engraved on the fibres of my brain, as the materialists would say? In that case, I should be powerless to modify it by my imagination and will. As I made these reflections, I had broken the branch, and I now tore off the lilac head. As I broke off each piece, I noticed how the appearance of the spray, as it became progressively smaller, still remained clearly and precisely what it would have been if I had done this in reality. When there remained no more than a very small cluster of lilac flowers, I wondered: shall I finish this illusory act of destruction, or shall I call a halt at this last modification of the original image? I venture to say that this depended entirely on a free decision on my part. But at that moment I awoke. (Quoted in Charles

McCreery, *Psychical Phenomena and the Physical World*, Hamish Hamilton, 1973, p. 89.)

> . . . I dreamt that I was out riding in fine weather. I became aware of my true situation, and remembered the question of whether or not I could exercise free will in controlling my actions in a dream. 'Well now,' I said to myself, 'This horse is only an illusion; this country-side that I am passing through is merely stage-scenery. But even if I have not evoked these images by conscious volition, I certainly seem to have some control over them. I decide to gallop, I gallop; I decide to stop, I stop. Now here are two roads in front of me. The one on the right appears to plunge into a dense wood; the one on the left leads to some kind of ruined manor. I feel quite distinctly that I am free to turn either right or left, and so to decide for myself whether I wish to produce images relating to the ruins or images relating to the wood.' I began by taking the right-hand road, but then it occurred to me that as this was such a clear dream it would be more interesting from the experimental point of view to dream of riding past the turrets and keep of the manor. I could then try to memorise the principal details of the architecture, and see if, when I awoke, I could recognise the memories on which they had been based. I therefore took the left-hand path, and dismounted by a picturesque drawbridge. For some time I very attentively examined numerous details of the manor's architecture: ogival arches, carved masonry, half-corroded pieces of ironwork, and fissures and alterations in the wall. I admired the minute precision with which all this was por-trayed. However, while I was still studying the gigantic lock of a dilapidated old door, everything suddenly faded and became blurred, like the figure of a diorama when it goes out of focus. I felt I was waking up. My eyes opened onto the real world, and the only light I could see was that from my night-light. It was three o'clock in the morning. (*Ibid.*, pp. 91–2.)

An out-of-the-body or ecsomatic experience is one in which the observer seems to himself to be observing the normal world from a point of view which is not coincident with that of his physical body. The following are two contrasting examples:

> Usually when visiting the dentist I had had cocaine for abstrac-tions.
> On two occasions my dentist prescribed gas.
> Never having experienced an anaesthetic before, I was terrified of taking it.
> I sat in the dentist chair, the dentist put his hand on my chest to gently push me back in the chair, and although I felt myself being pushed back, I found myself still sitting up (This was before the gas was given). I felt the solidity of my body lying back, the weight etc.,

yet here I was still sitting up. I got off the dentist chair and stood up some four feet away. I was astonished at what had happened to me! I had no feeling of weight, yet I could still feel the weight of my body in the chair!

I looked down at my second self and found myself to be a complete replica of my material self. I touched my clothes, and looked at myself and was astounded to see that I was wearing the same black skirt, white blouse with small red spots on it, same shoes etc., my reasoning power was quite normal as I was concerned as how I was to get back into myself again and if I ever would.

I watched and heard everything that was said and done. My husband who was with me at the time vouched for it when I eventually left the dentist.

I know that being unconscious in the dentist chair at the time, I would not have seen what was going on, as I was lying practically on my back.

I saw the dentist and the nurse with the dental instruments and cotton wool swabs etc:—which were arranged on a sort of bench against the wall opposite me. I also heard their conversation. But the view I got of them was not from the reclining position I was in, but from a normal standing position. In any case the reclining position I was in it would have been quite impossible for me to have seen this.

Also, I can remember them saying, 'She takes enough of this stuff to kill a person.'

I remember being terribly distressed and worried at the time as to how I was to get back into myself again.

However when I came out of the dentist chair I could not get out of the place quickly enough—as I was so anxious to explain to my husband what had happened to me. As I explained previously I was so *afraid* of having the 'Gas' my husband remained with me the whole time, and held my hand. So of course the first thing I asked him was, 'Are you quite sure my eyes were *closed* and that I was quite unconscious.' Also I asked him if the things I saw and heard actually happened. He said 'Yes.' I think we were both as stunned and mystified as each other.

I was working at Luton Airport as a fitter on nightshift, travelling by car to work from my home in Leighton Buzzard. After a shift of 7 p.m. to 7 a.m. I left work in that state of full wakefulness often experienced by night-workers after they survive the tiredness period of 2–4 a.m. Taking the Dunstable road I commenced dropping my passenger workmates at their homes. When Dunstable was reached only one remained, a Welsh lad living in Hockliffe on the A.5.

As Dunstable receded behind and we drove through more open country he called my attention to our surroundings. Overnight there had been an unusually heavy hoar frost of the white variety and now it covered every leaf, grass, tree branch and telegraph wire we passed. I paused at Hockliffe while my Welsh companion disembarked then turned off towards Leighton Buzzard with four miles of open country ahead before reaching my objective.

Having no distractions to occupy my attention I gazed around me, only giving the road an occasional glance. With a feeling of surprise and interest I discovered I had left my body and was now above it, travelling in company with the car and its contents but barely aware of their existence. The height I had attained brought my stomach to the level of the car roof through which my conscious centre—the head—and the upper part of my being had passed. Immediately upon realising this I also became aware of a considerable change in sensory perception. I now possessed one super-sense whose function-ing was immensely superior to that of my former five. Employing it I found that without turning I was aware of everything around me in a full circle of 360° to the distance of the horizon.

The surface of the ground was no barrier to this sense, it could penetrate solids with ease. With the greatest interest and satisfaction I studied the surrounding country which had undergone a subtle transformation. The fields and hedgerows, trees and slopes were those I was familiar with, yet they were changed in a way that eludes description rendering them most unfamiliar.

I had no further interest in my physical body, or indeed my physical life. I only wanted to pursue and prolong this happy state of being where everything was more bright, vivid and real than anything I had previously known.

Upon reaching the outskirts of Leighton Buzzard a farmhouse building came into sight with the red, yellow and brown brickwork unaffected by the frost and contrasting with the all-pervading crystalline whiteness that had prevailed up to this stage. Upon sight-ing it I promptly sank back down into my body, physical sensation returning, and taking charge of the controls once more I reached home.

The following are two examples of apparitional experiences:

It happened about eleven years ago, one Sunday evening. I was alone, sitting knitting and listening to a talk on the radio. Suddenly I was aware of my husband standing at the side of my chair. He looked white and drawn and was gazing straight ahead. It seemed strange to me afterwards that I did not speak because at the time I really thought it was my husband come home, coming in so quietly that because of my concentration on my knitting and radio, I had not heard him. As I looked up at him, he raised his arm and his hand came to rest under my chin and it felt *icy cold*. I shrank back in my chair from the chill feeling of it and the arm then fell back to his side. When I straightened up again, again he raised his arm, but this time I shrank back before his hand touched me. Then as I still looked up at him, he disappeared. Only then, did I realize that my husband had never been physically in the room. I am not a widow, so even if I believed the spirit of loved ones could return (and I am not a Spiritualist) that could not be the explanation.

The second case is taken from a letter from the percipient, Miss Grieve, to the well-known author Andrew Lang.

Skelfhill, Hawick, N.B., *August 8th*, 1906.

. . . I have been staying here since August 4th. On Monday, 6th, I went up the Pen and for the first time in my life saw a 'ghost!' Turk, the old Dandie Dinmont, was with me. Turk and I went very slowly, taking many rests on account of his short legs and shorter breath, and the grass and the brackens were long and strong. Our last stop was where the Pen suddenly takes up for its rocky top very steeply. I sat with my back against the dyke facing the steep part, and Turk lay panting beside me. I was thinking of a beautiful cleck-ing of grouse we had just disturbed—the two parent birds and five young ones clapped about four yards from us. Turk did not see them at first and I stood perfectly still watching, they were so pretty. Then Turk winded them and threw up his head, and of course with the movement the birds were off like a whirlwind. This just to show you my train of thought. Quite suddenly I saw coming along at right angles to me, a friend, Dr. H., who crossed with me May, 1905, from America. She was in a rather short dark blue skirt, white cotton blouse, no hat, and a stick in her hand—and later, I noticed a tail of hair beginning to 'come down.' I had heard about a fortnight ago that she had landed in England from America and was to sail back Sept. 12, and that she was going to her home in Cornwall for part of the time—but when I did not know. I was so surprised I did not say anything for a second or two till Turk began to growl. Then I jumped up exclaiming 'Dr. H.!' She looked straight at me, but when I spoke, turned and went on down the hill—following her own direc-tion and the one from which I had come. I followed quickly to catch her up, feeling rather queer because she did not speak, and *I knew she had seen me*! Turk barked and growled the whole time, but kept close to my heels and would not run out as he usually does at strange people or strange dogs. His hair was all on end and his tail hooked over his back, as stiff as a poker. I almost caught up Dr. H., and was just going to put out my hand to touch her shoulder, when a big bumble bee whirled between us and flew *right through* Dr. H. and she disappeared.

I certainly did feel queer after that—I was so very sure it was she and it was such a shock to find there was nothing. Had it not been for Turk I should have doubted my senses; but he was so un-mistakeably disturbed and angry. (*Journal of the S.P.R.*, Vol. XIII, 1907-8, pp. 28-9.)

(The percipient later learnt that at the time of her experience

Dr. H. was coming down a hill at Tintagel in the clothes she saw, but with a wet bathing-gown on her arm.)

Although the phenomenon of apparitions, unlike those of lucid dreams and out-of-the-body experiences, might appear to have been thoroughly worked over already by persons of high academic status and some intelligence (two factors which do not necessarily occur together), practically all the points made in our book on the subject,[1] and certainly all those of the greatest theoretical interest, had never been made before.

This is because the human race is unable to think straight in any area which reminds it of the possibility that the external world may be illusory. Lucid dreams and out-of-the-body experiences do so unmistakably and hence were ignored. Apparitions, it was thought, could be regarded in the light of quasi-physical entities or discarnate personalities popping in and out of a firmly concrete world.

*

We have proposed the term *metachoric experiences* to denote all those experiences in which the subject's normal surroundings are completely replaced by a hallucinatory environment. This class of phenomena had never been recognised before.

It may not be immediately obvious why the two apparition cases we have quoted in this chapter should be regarded as metachoric experiences like the lucid dreams and ecsomatic experiences, since the percipients were apparently seeing their normal environment, only with a hallucinatory figure superimposed upon it. However, the position is that we know for certain that some apparitional experiences are metachoric (for example the case quoted on p. 134 in which the percipient saw the apparition through closed eyelids), and we do not know for certain that any apparitional experiences are not. In our book *Apparitions* we discuss the possibility that in fact all apparitional experiences are of the metachoric variety, even though in many cases the environment containing the apparitional figure appears to be the subject's normal environment. Thus, in the last case quoted it may be that Miss Grieve was seeing a hallucinatory replica of the landscape in front of her while she was perceiving the apparition, this replica being very

[1] Celia Green and Charles McCreery, *Apparitions*, Hamish Hamilton, London, 1975.

similar to the landscape she would have been seeing in the normal way.

Of the three kinds of metachoric experience we have illustrated, lucid dreams and out-of-the-body experiences, which would lend themselves pre-eminently to further investigation, had been almost completely ignored before this Institute's investigations of them (and come to that still are being), even by persons interested in the study of parapsychology. It is, of course, not at all clear why interest in these phenomena should not be shown by psychologists and physiologists at large, since their interest is in no way dependent on the elements of extra-sensory perception which they sometimes contain. This, no doubt, accounts in some measure for the total disinterest with which the phenomena have been regarded.

The phenomenon of apparitions has been easier to regard as a specialised field which could only interest parapsychologists. This, of course, only holds water on the most superficial view, since on examination it is found that the phenomenon of apparition-seeing is only part of a generalised tendency on the part of the human race towards hallucinations of every variety. Even if this were not so, and the only hallucinations seen by sane and normal people were hallucinations of deceased relatives, the perceptual mechanisms involved should still be of the most general scientific interest. However, apparitions do not offer themselves so readily to investigation as do the related phenomena of lucid dreams and out-of-the-body experiences. This, no doubt, is another reason why it has been felt safe to give them a limited degree of highly selective attention.

The states of consciousness and the perceptual mechanisms involved in hallucinations of the sane are not accessible to direct examination for the simple reason that people experience them rarely and unpredictably, and no one appears to learn to have these experiences at will. However, the perceptual mechanisms involved are shown just as well in out-of-the-body experiences, and these are wide open to investigation, since all that is needed is a well-equipped electrophysiological laboratory in the hands of a motivated investigator. Those subjects who have these experiences habitually show no reluctance to take part in investigation, if the necessary finance should be forthcoming.

The tendency to ignore completely phenomena in which only the lack of resources in the hands of a motivated person can prevent advances in knowledge being made, in favour of phenomena which, taken alone, do in fact constitute something of a dead end, demonstrates the desire of those, both within and without the subject of parapsychology, to draw attention only to problems which there is little risk of being able to solve.

CHAPTER 11

Lucid Dreams

BLEULER, the inventor of the term *schizophrenia*, devoted some hundreds of pages to the attempt to define a satisfactory criterion for distinguishing between schizophrenic people and normal people. Finally, he was able to produce only two—thought-disorder and flattening of affect. These have remained ever since the standard characteristics by which schizophrenia is to be recognised.

However, both of these may be observed in certain forms in anybody. In particular, symptoms of thought-disorder can readily be elicited by anyone who makes a few logical or analytical observations of a certain kind. It should be noted in passing how seldom normal human conversation, even among intellectuals, is of any degree of analyticalness. Most commonly, it takes the form of exchanging truncated tags of association. For example, if you attempt to discuss with anybody what they mean by mysticism or religion you are liable to find that you have pressed the button which produces the response 'way of life'. It is virtually impossible to get any further.

The irrationality of most human utterance is not noticed simply because everyone is observing the same rules. They are all accepting the same vague and unspoken, but rock-hard, beliefs and they are all deriving social support by exchanging these unanalysed and loosely associated allusive phrases.

If, however, one breaks the rules of the game and attempts to speak about things which do not directly contribute to the maintenance of the general stock of social beliefs, it is very easy to elicit symptoms of thought-disorder.

For example, the idea of lucid dreams—dreams in which the subject is aware that he is dreaming—is not an acceptable one.

Perhaps this is particularly true in the case of recognised intellectuals who know (although of course they never say this explicitly) that the idea of someone thinking rationally while they are asleep does not fit in with the way in which they would like to think about human consciousness and the human brain. I have discovered by experiment that if you attempt to discuss the phenomenon of lucid dreams with leading intellectuals, who may be experts in some field such as neurophysiology, you will find them to have the greatest seeming difficulty in remembering the definition of a lucid dream from one sentence to another. The definition of a lucid dream is, I repeat, that it is one in which the dreamer is continually aware that he is dreaming. Naturally, you state this definition very clearly at the outset, but after a little while you are liable to find that the person to whom you are talking has seemingly forgotten this definition, and is talking as if what is in question is precognitive dreams, or extremely vivid dreams, or narrative dreams.

Here, by way of illustration, is part of a lucid dream:

> As I walk along, knowing perfectly clearly that I am dreaming, I think about M. Maury's ideas. I wonder what part of my brain he would say was awake at this time. He should certainly consider, I say to myself, that my entire cerebrum is in a waking state, for it is my definite opinion that at this moment I am in full possession of my intellectual faculties; I feel that I am able to think rationally and to remember. What I have read about materialistic theories and what I wish to observe in connection with this dream presents itself very clearly to my mind!
>
> I even reason as follows: the images which appear to me in this dream are no more imposed upon me than the images which present themselves to my eyes when I am awake. I retain as well as usual my freedom of choice to turn right or left, to direct my eyes in one direction or in another, and so on. Indeed, I can summon up certain scenes or produce certain images accordingly as I wish or do not wish to act mentally as a result of what I see. For example: if I want to break a branch of one of these trees which I seem to see, the branch will seem to be broken. If I do not want this to happen the branch will continue to look unbroken to me. How does the dream differ for me from reality? I remember, I reason, I will, I do not will: I am not the helpless victim of the hallucination in which I am involved. If my acts of volition are not followed by real efforts, this is only because, instead of my physical organs obeying my thought, only an image of this process takes place; but the psychological phenomenon is exactly the same. (The Marquis d'Hervey de Saint-Denys, quoted in my book *Lucid Dreams*, Hamish Hamilton, 1968, p. 92; my translation.)

Now personally I do not see why lucid dreams should be found so emotionally disturbing; but clearly they are. What modern intellectuals feel is the right kind of thing to believe about the human brain is that it is some kind of computer, which can only run efficiently while it is being used for the purpose of interacting with the physical environment. When a person is asleep (so I have heard it said) the computer-brain, deprived of stimuli from the outer world, behaves like a computer switched off or functioning purely at random. I might have regarded this as a mere casual speculation, seeing that in fact there is little direct evidence to support such a view of the matter, were it not for the highly significant irrationality shown by so many people in the presence of the idea of lucid dreams. This reveals that what might be thought a vague speculation is actually an expression of some kind of profound dogmatic belief, and that there are deep-seated emotional reasons which render it necessary for people *not* to recognise that lucid dreams happen.

Here is another example of a lucid dream:

> I was involved in a sort of Passion Play thing; set-up much like a cinema, me sitting in front row of circle and looking towards a sort of cathedral facade with some kind of diabolical court going on in it—galleries of people within the facade. Knew that I was cast as Christ and they would get round to killing me eventually. However I knew it was a dream and felt cheerful, so I sat reflecting on the remarkable elaboration of the cathedral-like structure (which included metal ornamentation) and on how good lucid dreams were at this sort of thing. Also replied with some jollity to a question from the chief inquisitor/devil, who leaned out of his gallery to address me across the auditorium. It did occur to me that one might feel apprehensive about the killing, and I wondered if I could (a) get out of the building or (b) wake up—but really only an academic question whether to not to cultivate apprehension. It didn't seem appropriate so I went on with the jolly cheerfulness. Then there was a break in proceedings and I found myself off-stage under escort. (The whole auditorium seemed to be 'on-stage'—'off-stage' was not proper dressing-rooms but a very informal living-room set-up. Informal though it was, the people sitting round weren't friendly but there to keep an eye on me, though they seemed not to be paying me any attention.) I considered what I was wearing and thought I would like a doublet and hose, so made them appear beside me and put them on. Saw someone watching materialisation of the clothes with some surprise and thought they had no idea how easy it really was in a dream.

Let us now consider some examples which will serve to

illustrate the fact that lucid dreams are a completely different
psychological phenomenon from ordinary dreams.

For example, the emotional quality of lucid dreams is quite
different from that of ordinary dreams, and the following case
illustrates an emotional detachment in an alarming situation which
is very characteristic of lucid dreams.[1]

> In ordinary dream was trying to get on a bus which I was chasing
> along the road, dodging in and out of traffic and holding a ribbon
> which connected me to the bus. This ribbon seemed to be elastic and
> I noticed with annoyance that it was elongating and I was falling
> behind. Then I realised I was dreaming and did not need to chase the
> bus or even to dodge the traffic. So I stopped running and stood still
> in the road—the traffic vanishing as I did so. Then I thought that I
> would go wherever my subconscious liked to take me. I floated into
> a horizontal position, some four or five feet above the ground, and
> floated along.
>
> Soon I found myself in a cave with ornamental rocky pools, in
> which were goldfish and small frogs. The place seemed to be electric-
> ally lighted—there was a clear glistening texture to the wet rocks and
> the frogs. I walked about a bit, looking at things, and then went up a
> staircase in the rock. This was a winding stair—not tight enough to
> be called spiral—and came out on a rocky balcony. Then I heard
> shouting and found that there were some hostile people about. A
> sort of pirate man came bounding up the stairs from the cave below
> and emerged on to the balcony, looking fierce and throwing knives
> at me (I was standing by the parapet). I thought that as this was a
> dream I was perfectly safe, and anyway dreams could be controlled.
> I thought the thing to do would be to call on some Higher Power,
> which surely should in some way eliminate the inconvenience. I
> tried mentally to do this, but nothing happened. Felt vaguely re-
> buffed and inadequate, but still not worried, because I thought that
> even if he hit me the knives would only go straight through and
> couldn't hurt or damage me at all. (Incidentally, on reflection after
> the event, his aim was being extraordinarily bad at about two yards
> range.) Still, I thought I would get away from him, so I stepped over
> the edge of the balcony and lay down comfortably on the air, intend-
> ing to float away—but there the dream ended.

The following case illustrates the kind of analytical thinking
characteristic of lucid dreams, in contrast to the irrational kinds of
association of ideas that tend to occur in ordinary dreams:

> First I was having an ordinary dream in which I seemed to be
> walking along some corridors in a vaguely institutional large building,

[1] See Chapter 14 of my book *Lucid Dreams*.

and I thought I wanted to go to the lavatory. I was sufficiently aware that I was dreaming to think I had better wake up to do this, and the scene then changed to a rather different set of institutional corridors. I then tried to decide whether this had constituted a genuine waking up. I partly remembered the criterion that if one is not sure whether one is awake or not, one must be dreaming. But I did not manage to formulate this very clearly to myself. The question of deciding by reference to the reality of the surroundings went on seeming much more immediate and concrete. The difficulty in formulating the abstract criterion may be because there is an emotional resistance to realising this, or it may just be that I had not formulated it clearly enough to myself in the waking state. This is the kind of point which, if one fails to get right in a lucid dream and then thinks about in the waking state, one often gets more clearly in a subsequent lucid dream. Anyway I went on looking at the surroundings and thinking that there was no way of distinguishing them from real life, so after a time I decided simply to accept that I could not tell whether I was awake or asleep and went on walking through these corridors. After a time, I thought, 'I have been going on some time now and none of this building is familiar to me, nor can I relate it to any place that is familiar to me, and so I must be dreaming.' Well after that all that happened was that I continued walking around this place, knowing that I was dreaming, until eventually I suppose the dream lapsed back into an ordinary one.

I was a bit intellectually passive throughout this prelucid dream, as if tired, but this may be because I have not been deliberately trying to get lucid dreams recently and had no particular intentions about what I should try to do if I had one.

There seems to be in human psychology some quite distinct emotional resistance to recognising lucid dreams. Of states of consciousness containing the potentiality for ESP they are one of the easiest for any reasonably determined person to obtain. Since it is one of the characteristics of lucid dreams that they do not contain the grotesque, confused or frightening elements of ordinary dreams, and since they offer opportunities for quite a variety of realistic and agreeable experiences, it would seem that cultivating them might be attractive. Yet remarkably few people are known to have done so prior to the studies made at the Institute of Psychophysical Research, and even those few have not declared explicitly that this was a phenomenon quite distinct from ordinary dreaming, which deserved to be studied in its own right. And, as we have already mentioned, many people may be found to experience actual difficulty in remembering the definition of a lucid dream from one sentence to the next. It seems to follow that human psychology has some vested interest in rejecting the phenomenon, which might otherwise seem to offer access to varied nocturnal entertainments, with no perceptible draw-backs. For example, in the following two cases the lucid dreamers experiment with the sense of taste in lucid dreams:

> In the background of the dream-scene I saw a street which I recognised as one in Seville, where I had not been for ten years. I immediately remembered that there was a very famous ice-cream shop round the corner of this street. I was curious to know how my memory would acquit itself if I tried guiding my dream in this direction, and set off accordingly. I perceived the shop with minute distinctness, and recognised in it all sorts of little cakes of characteristic shapes. Among the other refreshments were some hazel-nut water ices, something which I had never come across elsewhere. I then reflected that this was a valuable opportunity to see whether I could recall a taste as faithfully as I recalled visual images. I chose one of these imaginary water-ices, and raised it to my lips, concentrating all my attention on tasting it. I realised that my memory had failed me and was only providing me with an approximation to the sensation which was required of it. What it produced was an almond taste, and not a hazel-nut taste. I woke up immediately by an effort of will, in order to make a note of this. (The Marquis d'Hervey de Saint-Denys, quoted in Charles McCreery, *Psychical Phenomena and the Physical World*, pp. 89–90.)

> Strolling along in some seaside resort I realised it was a dream. The sea looked dull, which struck me as most unusual for a lucid dream, although I noticed a glow developing to the east. I gazed down at the beach far below, and considered jumping, but demurred at the thought of the unpleasant falling sensation, which would doubtless be real enough although I knew I could not hurt myself. I walked on until I came to a path, which I descended. Noisy band music was playing, and I became aware of a cool breeze—a definite thermal sensation I reflected, and decided to investigate other effects. On reaching the lower promenade I tried hitting my leg with a stick; the sensation felt fairly realistic on the first stroke, but diminished to nil thereafter. I paddled in the sea, noting the coolness of the waves. My next aim was a gustatory sensation. Espying a jar of smallish (raw) plums on a counter I took one and began eating. The yellow flesh had a distinct plum flavour, although not quite as intense as one would expect in waking experience. While still eating (the plum increasing in size) I awoke, precluding any seeking of olfactory sensations.

One might think that it would be attractive to acquire the ability to have agreeable and varied nocturnal experiences of this kind, and it is remarkable that a knowledge of lucid dreaming has never become an accepted feature of human culture. Evidently some emotional force is at work which takes precedence over the pleasure principle.

Does the emotional resistance to developing lucid dreams reside in the fact that skill at lucid dreaming is acquired by the cultivation of awareness? There is some indication that it is those who are most in the habit of thinking critically about the state of their consciousness, and their relation to their environment, who are most likely to develop prolific lucid dreams. The development of a detached and critical attitude towards one's own mind and the circumstances of one's life is scarcely what the human race seems most eager to cultivate.

Alternatively, is the emotional resistance to the idea of lucid dreams based upon the fact that they can provide environments in every respect as realistic as those of waking life, and that the dreamer can experience these seemingly with his wits about him as completely as if he were awake? Perhaps people do not like to be reminded of the philosophical possibility that life may be hallucinatory. This possibility has, of course, often been touched upon by philosophers, but usually with some signs of emotional disturbance in themselves or their opponents.

Berkeley no sooner formulated the idea that the world might be illusory (a perfectly valid statement of a possibility) than he felt impelled to follow it with a dogmatic solution in which God was invoked to ensure the permanency of the external world and its independence of human observers.

As a matter of fact, the study of lucid dreams should suffice to invalidate some of the supposed refutations of the illusory nature of the external world which have been made.[1] The study of lucid dreams should not, of course, be necessary to demonstrate the invalidity of these arguments.

Consider Dr. Samuel Johnson's celebrated 'refutation' of Berkeley, as described by Boswell:

> After we came out of the church, we stood talking for some time together of Bishop Berkeley's ingenious sophistry to prove the non-existence of matter, and that every thing in the universe is merely

[1] For a discussion of the philosophical implications of lucid dreams see *Psychical Phenomena and the Physical World* by my colleague Charles McCreery, Chapter I.

ideal. I observed, that though we are satisfied his doctrine is not true, it is impossible to refute it. I never shall forget the alacrity with which Johnson answered, striking his foot with mighty force against a large stone, till he rebounded from it, 'I refute it *thus*.' (*Everybody's Boswell*, Bell, 1930, p. 99.)

Dr. Johnson was not a philosopher and therefore it might be said he did not know any better. However, similar arguments are put forward even by professional philosophers. Consider, for example, Professor Broad, who incidentally knew of the existence of lucid dreams, which makes his attitude even more remarkable:

> My own tentative view is that tactual perception . . . justifies us in being practically certain that there are foreign bodies and that they do interact with our own bodies. It seems to me just conceivable, though extremely unlikely, that I might have had the kinds of experience which I describe as 'seeing' or 'hearing' foreign bodies even if there had been no foreign bodies or if they had never emitted light-waves or sound-waves to my body. But I find it almost impossible to believe I could *ever* have had the kind of experience which I describe as 'pushing' or 'pulling' or 'struggling with' foreign bodies unless there had been foreign bodies and they had *quite often* interacted dynamically with my own body through contact. (C. D. Broad, *Religion, Philosophy and Psychical Research*, Routledge & Kegan Paul, 1953, p. 34.)

The fact that such arguments have been seriously entertained is so much the more evidence that human psychology has emotional conflicts in this region which prevent clearness of thought. This may be part of the reason why lucid dreams have remained a neglected human potentiality, and why it is so difficult even now to induce people to remember how they are defined, let alone contribute money for research on them.

The Institute's study of lucid dreams was the first which had ever been made of this phenomenon. Previously a few people had published accounts of their own lucid dreams, but no one had recognised or studied the phenomenon in general. While our work on lucid dreams has revealed a good deal concerning the characteristics of this state of consciousness, our work on them now requires laboratory facilities before it can be carried further.

*

Lucid dreams are among those states in which extrasensory perception is reported. Naturally, this leads to the result that people cannot discuss the question of research on them without assuming that what you have in mind is to 'prove' the existence of extrasensory perception by means of lucid dreams. As a matter of fact, if I had the financial resources to do research on lucid dreams, while I should certainly not neglect opportunities to study the phenomenon of extrasensory perception at the same time, I should primarily wish to find out the psychological and physiological characteristics of lucid dreams as a phenomenon in their own right. It would not disturb me very much if they turned out to have characteristics in some respects very close to those of waking life, and in others very close to those of normal dreaming. However, I should like to know what these characteristics are, and it seems to me that science in general should also want to know.

Lucid dreams are not studied except by those with an interest in parapsychology. On the face of it, this might seem strange, since the interest of lucid dreams is quite independent of the fact that subjects sometimes report the occurrence of telepathic communications in them. If all these reports were rejected, the case for studying lucid dreams would still be just as strong.

This, of course, is why they are not studied. All phenomena of an inconvenient kind are tarred with the 'paranormal' brush and abandoned to the parapsychologists. It should not be supposed that the parapsychologists study lucid dreams to more than an insignificant extent. They study them in fact so little that it is scarcely meaningful to discuss their approach to doing so, but when one discusses with them the kind of work which they might, in the most abstract and hypothetical way, one day think of doing, it is clear that their ideas in this direction are rigorously limited to studying them in the least effective way. If they were to insist on the importance of the phenomenon as such, and to study it in its own right, nothing but motivated ineptitude could prevent them from making definite discoveries concerning the nature and conditions of this state of consciousness, and the way it is related to other, quite different states of consciousness, such as being normally awake or having common or garden dreams. If such information were to be produced by research, only dishonesty and evasiveness could prevent orthodox scientists from regarding it as distinct and significant scientific information.

However, parapsychologists are social animals with a social conscience, and they do not want to make it inconveniently difficult for society to ignore their work. So, in the case of lucid dreams as in the case of all other similar phenomena, what would naturally occur to the minds of almost all parapsychologists would be to devote any energy and attention which they should ever bestow upon them (with the restrictiveness but scarcely the driving force of monomania) to seeing whether evidence for the existence of telepathy could be produced in them. If such evidence happened to be forthcoming in their experiments, they would be confident that it could be ignored on the same terms as all the other evidence for the existence of telepathy which had been produced previously. It would not, of course, have any claim to be a repeatable experiment, since if telepathy were observed at all it would be a purely accidental consequence of the fact that it sometimes occurs in lucid dreams, and no one would be able to say if it would happen on another occasion. The conditions of occurrence, if any, would not be studied in any way which would enable conclusions to be drawn about the conditions of occurrence of ESP, or even the conditions of occurrence of lucid dreams. If observations of this kind were made, a genuinely repeatable experiment might, in fact almost certainly would, become possible. However, parapsychologists are considerate and do not wish to inconvenience society.

*

Darwin once made the point that scientists had an emotional tendency to forget any facts they came across which did not fit in with their preferred theories. He recommended that scientists should make a particularly careful note, in writing, of facts which ran counter to their preconceptions, as they were otherwise so likely to slip from the mind. Modern intellectuals do not take much notice of advice of this kind. Far from paying extra attention to indications that things may not be exactly as they like to believe them, they seem to feel they have a moral obligation to shun anything which does not fit with the socially acceptable beliefs which they hold. In this, of course, they are assisted by the fact that their dogmatic beliefs are never explicitly stated.

In the case of lucid dreaming, one might think that the paradoxical nature of the phenomenon would make a thorough investigation of it particularly interesting. It might be thought that it would be interesting to discover what the neurophysiological state of a person was when their mind was in a state of rational activity although they were physically asleep. If this state should turn out to be exactly the same as that of a person who was asleep and dreaming in the ordinary irrational manner, this would be strange and interesting. If it should turn out to be different, the nature of the differences might shed light on the true nature of sleep and the true nature of rational mental functioning.

It is of course impossible to demonstrate to anyone who does not wish to be convinced that something is wide open to investigation. An old-fashioned proverb, no longer perhaps very fashionable, was to the effect that you could take a horse to water but you could not make him drink. The Roman Catholic Church has, I believe, a concept of invincible ignorance. Discussing the prospects for research in this field with members of the human race is likely to make one believe in invincible stupidity.

'What have lucid dreams to do with science?' they ask, in an attitude of witless open-mindedness, expressive of their perfect willingness to allow you to talk yourself into exhaustion. 'Just exactly how would you set about it? What do you mean by finding things out? And what exactly would you find out?'

It is, of course, true that lucid dreams have nothing to do with science in the sense of the system of beliefs which assists in the maintenance of the modern world-view. But what the invincible stupidity of the human race really demonstrates is that research of any genuinely progressive kind (that is, which involves the discovery of new facts sufficiently at variance with accepted dogma to compel revision of it) can never, contrary to modern dogmatic belief, be carried out by committees or under any analogous form of collective management. Unfashionable as the concept of an individual is, and reprehensible though that of an exceptional individual may be, it is as true as it has ever been that significant advances in knowledge depend upon them.

CHAPTER 12

Out-of-the-Body Experiences

IT is discouraging in the extreme to recount to someone several
striking examples of out-of-the-body experiences, and to find him
maintain a somewhat resistant expression until you tell him of a
case which appears to contain an element of extra-sensory perception, such as the following:

> I was in hospital having had an operation for peritonitis; I
> developed pneumonia and was very ill. The ward was L shaped; so
> that anyone in bed at one part of the ward, could not see round the
> corner.
> One morning I felt myself floating upwards, and found I was
> looking down on the rest of the patients. I could see myself; propped
> up against pillows, very white and ill. I saw the sister and nurse rush
> to my bed with oxygen. Then everything went blank. The next I
> remember; was opening my eyes to see the sister bending over me.
> I told her what had happened; but at first she thought I was
> rambling. Then I said, 'There is a big woman sitting up in bed with
> her head wrapped in bandages; and she is knitting something with
> blue wool. She has a very red face.' This certainly shook her; as
> apparently; the lady concerned had a mastoid operation and was just
> as I described.
> She was not allowed out of bed; and of course I hadn't been up at
> all. After several other details; such as the time by the clock on the
> wall (which had broken down) I convinced her that at least something
> strange had happened to me.

On hearing a case such as this your interlocutor will then say,
brightening, 'Now that *is* interesting.' Here we confront the deter-
mination of the human race to find it totally uninteresting and un-
worthy of further investigation that someone can perceive the
world quite accurately and informatively, but from a position
which, seemingly, does not coincide with that of their physical
eyes. This is presumably because investigation of this phenomenon

would be an extremely simple matter, and could hardly fail to affect our views on the nature and mechanisms of sensory perception. In other words, if the phenomenon of ecsomatic experiences is accepted as paradoxical in its own right, the way stands open to further research, particularly as it is not difficult to find subjects who have these experiences more or less at will. All that is needed is an electrophysiological laboratory in the hands of someone who wishes to find something out. The latter proviso has to be made, because there is no doubt that the most elaborate facilities in the hands of the unmotivated (even if the unmotivated are perfectly respectable and qualified persons) can lead to absolutely no distinct advance in information.

If, however, the position is adopted that out-of-the-body experiences are only interesting in so far as they contain highly evidential pieces of telepathy, and it is further implied that the study of ecsomatic experiences as a phenomenon in their own right can only be undertaken once it has been demonstrated to universal satisfaction that they contain telepathy in overwhelming quantity and of irrefutable quality, research faces a brick wall. In fact, it faces the familiar brick wall with which people like to confront all research in this subject. It is completely impossible to convince people that they are compelled to accept the evidence for telepathy. However energetically and assiduously one were to collect the best, and most perfectly corroborated, examples of extrasensory perception occurring in out-of-the-body experiences, and in all the other types of state as well in which ESP sometimes occurs, this would still be inadequate to convince anyone who did not wish to be convinced. It would also, incidentally, be very expensive; and part of the social technique for ignoring this subject is to ensure that those who might wish to do it with an inconvenient degree of pertinacity are kept extremely short of money.

As we know, the would-be tolerant and open-minded individual, when told of a strikingly evidential piece of ESP, or a striking experimental result, says, 'Well, I am surprised to hear that,' or 'How fascinating,' and then, 'Why don't you do it again?' He never offers to get you the finance which would be needed to repeat the expensive work already done, or better still, to carry it one stage further.

*

In parapsychology there is a concept of a 'break-through'. It is generally agreed, by those who know anything at all about the subject, that what it needs is a 'break-through'. It seems to be implied that once this break-through has been made, the world will become unanimously convinced of the reality of paranormal phenomena, and research will be able to go ahead in a socially approved manner, under the auspices of large institutions and committees, in a way that will require no particular exercise of initiative on the part of any individual.

This is, of course, a completely implausible scenario. In the first place, it is necessary to distinguish between a break-through in the sense of an actual advance in knowledge, and a break-through in the sense of a change in attitude on the part of an effective majority of the population.

A break-through of the second kind has no necessary relation with the first. It is impossible to defeat motivation. Galileo was unable to convince his inquisitors that the earth moved round the sun, not because his observations were defective or his reasoning less than cogent, but simply because they were motivated to look at the matter in a quite different light. The human race has already demonstrated its ability to ignore successive pieces of evidence that extrasensory perception and psychokinesis occur. It has also demonstrated its ability to remain in total ignorance of states such as lucid dreaming and out-of-the-body experiences which, if accepted, would be inconvenient for neurologists and physiologists to explain. I do not see any reason why the human race should not be able to shrug off any piece of evidence that any of these phenomena exist. It is, I repeat, impossible to defeat motivation.

As for break-throughs in the sense of advances of knowledge, there have already been several. This Institute has itself made several. What they have all failed to do is to kindle any desire to take the matter further. No evidence of paranormal phenomena seems to arouse any desire to find out more, no matter how obvious it may be that more could be found out in relatively simple ways. Nor does it arouse any desire to finance those who would be interested in finding out more by pursuing the lines of research which obviously present themselves.

One receives the impression that until the break-through has been made, in the sense that the study of paranormal phenomena *en bloc* receives unanimous social approval, no one will feel at all right about doing it. What is done must be done with diffidence, and the thoughts of research workers must never stray from their prime task of offering to the social divinity pieces of evidence that it should be done at all.

This cult of the evidential has distorted and restricted the study of the phenomena. For example, the only out-of-the-body experiences which investigators have found interesting were those in which the subject saw things which he could not normally have seen, and in which corroboration could be obtained from other people. So a few cases of this kind were placed on record, which the human race at large ignored as successfully as usual, and which were then left well alone to age into oblivion.

Now it may well be the case that extrasensory perception sometimes happens in out-of-the-body experiences, and this extrasensory perception is sometimes sufficiently detailed, and corroborated in sufficient detail by a sufficient number of people, to warm the cockles of the evidentialist's heart. But these cases are only a small minority of those reported, and it might seem sufficiently remarkable in itself that people should quite commonly have experiences of the ecsomatic type to justify further investigation.

Indeed, why should one be so interested in whether ecsomatic experiences sometimes contain evidence of high quality for the existence of extrasensory perception? Evidence of equally good quality is provided in many other places, and if that has failed to arouse investigatory zeal there is no reason why adding to it some pieces of evidence of a similar kind, but with the added distinction of having occurred in out-of-the-body experiences, should succeed.

*

What is disturbing to the modern world-view about out-of-the-body experiences is that they are able to provide the subject with a complete perceptual environment, as clear and precise as his normal one, but apparently without his sensory apparatus being involved. Often this substitute environment is apparently identical with his real one at the time of the experience, but 'seen' from a different point of view. For example, in the following case the percipient seems to leave her body and see the same scene as she was perceiving just before the experience but from a position some hundred feet up in the air:

> A friend and I had travelled from Bedford to St. Albans in order to visit Verulamium. The day was warm, but not hot, one needed a jacket, and there was a slight breeze. When we got to an open, grassy place near to the amphitheatre we sat and ate some sandwiches and fresh apricots to quench our thirst. There were a few people about, but it was not crowded. After sitting and talking for a while we wandered on, talking. Suddenly I seemed to be 50–100 ft. above my body. I could see us both walking along in the shallow bowl of hills, and could see small gestures. I seemed to be floating along above myself rather like a balloon attached to a string, but I could not see how I was attached, rather I was conscious of moving along to keep pace with my body. My actual body had no sensation whatever and seemed as remote as that of my friend. Reality was my 'floating self' and the objects below seemed as shadows against the reality of my floating self. I could see, but could not hear what was going on. It was not frightening, it was peaceful, secure and right. Perhaps I was more conscious than I normally am, probably because it was a new experience. I think I wondered at it at the time. Suddenly I was back in myself. Going out and coming back was like the flick of a switch. During the whole period of time I had continued to walk. Whether I had carried on a conversation or not I could not say, nor do I know how long I was out. Possibly it was only momentary.

In addition to their unpleasant attribute of reminding people that the human mind can project a substitute environment, and consequently that the status of normal perception is not, on commonsense terms, too secure, out-of-the-body experiences have the unfortunate characteristic of appealing, when studied objectively, neither to the mechanical-computer type of materialist, nor to the spiritualist.

Even if the facts of ecsomatic experiences can be squared with some computer-like explanation of the functioning of the human nervous system, they would certainly require such a theory to have a few special clauses inserted in it to account for them. Of course, you may always continue to hold any desired theory, provided you are prepared to make it sufficiently complicated. However, human psychology does not wish its theories to become complicated. It is easier, as in this case, to ignore any facts which do not immediately support it in its crudest form.

Similarly, spiritualists would like everyone to possess a pseudo-physical spirit-body, identical with his physical one, and attached to it by a silver cord which is severed only on death. In most ecsomatic experiences the subject is not aware of a duplicate body at all, and when he is it is often very unlike his physical body. Silver cords are not much in evidence.

In the following two cases, for example, neither of the two percipients are provided with a duplicate 'body' which bears any resemblance to a human body. In the first the subject finds himself taking the form of a bird, and in the second the percipient does not occupy a 'body' at all:

> Years ago, my mother had once shown me a photo of the interior of the roof of Exeter Cathedral: she was a Devonian. She spoke of the wonderful soaring effect it had on one, but I had no liking for the picture—it seemed to me like the ribs of a skeleton as seen from inside.
> About 15 years or so later, a few years after my mother's death, I visited Exeter on my way to Truro for an interview. I had some time to wait for a connection at Exeter and I went into the Cathedral and sat down alone there, feeling sad and lonely as I have done often since my mother's death in 1950.
> Suddenly, I remembered that this was the cathedral with the wonderful roof—I looked up and instantly became a small sized greyish bird or creature of bird-like formation, working my wings to keep level with a beam or piece of structure just as one treads water when swimming sometimes. I smelt something dry and musty and saw, but I think not with eyes, dust in clumps, white and grey along this bar. I felt desolate, then realized that I was up in the roof. I looked down and saw the top of my brown felt hat and my hands loosely lying in my lap.

> I was in bed, it was summer, and I couldn't get to sleep, so I just relaxed, on my back, and thought of nothing in particular, just at peace with myself. After a time I decided to turn over and try to sleep, in doing so I felt a quick movement inside me, I seemed to be inside myself leaping up to get out. Next thing I know is that I'm near the ceiling in the corner of the room looking down on my body with my husband's next to it. At first I thought it very funny it couldn't be possible. I'm up here and yet I'm lying in bed down there. I wondered if I could wake my husband up but I seemed to have no hands to shake him or touch him, there was nothing of me all I could do is see. Then the thought struck me that I might be dead and I panicked. Immediately thinking that thought I slipped straight backed into my body as quickly as I had come out.

Most disturbing of all, to materialist and spiritualist alike, is the fact that what is seen by an ecsomatic subject is not always a perfect representation of the real world. It may contain elements of fantasy or unrealism which lead one to the view that the whloe thing is actually hallucinatory and not a 'real' perception, as people seem to wish to think. And yet what is seen during the experience may look as real as the world of normal perception, and may in almost all particulars be an accurate source of information about it.

The following case is one which embodies elements of unrealism: for example, the theatre 'visited' by the percipient during the ecsomatic experience had its stage the 'wrong' end of the auditorium:

> One very interesting experience occurred when, in this 'floating' state, I decided to project my conscious self some distance away from my body, and 'willed' myself to travel some two hundred miles, to visit a theatre in my home town, where I knew there was a production in which I was very much interested.
>
> Immediately the desire occurred, I was 'there', in the foyer of the theatre, and drifted towards the corridor which I knew led to the auditorium. To my surprise, everything appeared to be 'wrong way round': The stalls corridor was on the wrong side of the foyer, and the stage the wrong end of the auditorium, as I remember it.
>
> I drifted some feet above the heads of the audience, in an upright position (and obviously invisible) and was able quite clearly to see and hear the play which was proceeding on the stage. A significant point is that I am rather deaf and could never, in the body, have heard stage dialogue without my hearing-aid; nor could I have seen so perfectly without my glasses. Despite the absence of both these artificial aids, I found no difficulty whatever in seeing and hearing perfectly. . . .
>
> I was greatly enjoying the play and delighting in my unique method of seeing it (not without a slight feeling of rather smug satisfaction at my own 'cleverness'!!) when something on the stage amused me, and I began to laugh. Immediately I was back in my physical body, and found it, to my disappointment, impossible to return.[1]

---

[1] For further data on ecsomatic experiences see my book *Out-of-the-Body Experiences*. The reader will also find additional material in Charles McCreery's book *Psychical Phenomena and the Physical World*, Chapters 2, 8 and 9.

CHAPTER 13

Apparitions

AMONG those with no particular pretensions to expert knowledge in any direction, and certainly no claims to have studied the work that has been done on the phenomena, it is thought appropriate to treat the concept of 'apparitions' as identical with the concept of 'ghosts' in the popular sense. That is to say, the question whether people see things which are not there, including at times the figures of people, is treated as if it were identical with the theory that human personality survives death and goes on wandering around in a spirit world somehow related to our physical world, in which from time to time it puts in an appearance. It is held that you cannot believe the former of these things without being a firm believer in the latter, and thus qualifying for ridicule. It is, of course, difficult to proceed to a sensible discussion of apparitions and other hallucinations seen by sane people when it is thought right always to return the argument to square one, and to discuss whether it is not ridiculous to believe that they happen at all.

Of course, scepticism in the field of apparitions, as in connection with other phenomena which are treated as paranormal, is considerably aided by the fact that the work already done in these fields, although carried out by people of high academic qualifications and great experience as investigators, has never been allowed to become part of the general culture. Consequently each new investigator is treated as though he were the first, and everyone is astonished to learn that people actually do see apparitions. Then they allow his work to lapse into obscurity, so that when the next investigator comes along they may be astonished afresh.

However, although it certainly does appear to be unreasonable to doubt that a good many people do, from time to time, see things which are not there, including figures of human beings, this does not appear to me as a terminus but as a starting-point for investigation.

*

It is very common when a fundamental scientific advance is about to be made for people to think it is going to prove or disprove some dogmatic belief in a very direct way, and this greatly hinders it from being treated objectively. For example, the development of astronomy was greatly hindered because people thought it would disprove Christianity if the sun was found not to move round the earth, so everyone argued about their dogmatic beliefs instead of taking an objective interest in what might be the case. The same thing happened when Darwin suggested the idea of evolution. People thought that if they accepted evolution, this would also disprove Christianity, so the argument was conducted in very heated, emotional terms.

Once these discoveries have become part of accepted knowledge, people no longer find them of such direct dogmatic relevance.

In the same way it is very difficult to get people to take an objective interest in the phenomena which are called paranormal, which is really only a name for the phenomena that people have decided not to be objective about. For example, out-of-the-body experiences are supposed to have a very direct bearing on whether or not one is able to believe in survival. This means that people tend to discuss them very much in the context of a dogmatic belief one way or the other. If these things were known about in a much more extensive scientific context, I think it would come to seem much less obvious to take them as proving survival or anything of the sort, in the same way that few people any longer regard astronomy as a way of disproving Christianity.

In connection with our work on apparitions in particular we are always being asked whether we 'believe in ghosts', and the answer to this ill-defined question is supposed to have a very direct bearing on one's dogmatic beliefs or otherwise in the question of survival. Actually, this is rather like asking a modern chemist whether he 'believes' in the transmutation of base metals into gold as the alchemists did. Obviously he doesn't, but this does not mean that he does not believe that chemical reactions take place. There is even a sense in which he accepts that the transmutation of one metal into another is possible, by processes such as the well-known one in which uranium disintegrates into lead, with the release of radioactivity. However, he would find it difficult to explain his position exactly if he was always being asked whether he 'believed' in alchemy, and if he said he did not, it was taken as expressing a disbelief in chemical reactions.

In considering paranormal phenomena, people are always wanting to leap from the facts (which they rarely pause to examine in any detail) to the very direct and drastic consequence which these facts are supposed to have on their dogmatic beliefs about matters which are really very far-removed from a simple consideration of the facts.

This is not to say that the facts are not paradoxical and important. The finding that the earth went round the sun was the start of a new era of development in astronomy, but it was not important as evidence against a dogmatic belief in the existence of a Hell and Heaven after death.

*

People sometimes ask whether, when someone sees an apparition of a deceased person, what they see is exactly the same as really seeing the person. There is no doubt that when people discuss apparitions much of their thinking is conditioned by the idea of a 'spirit-body', which is an exact replica of the physical body. If it appears in our physical world, it is supposed, the spirit-body can be seen in much the same way as a normal physical body. Some elaborate theories have been evolved, and at times have been quite popular, describing how in addition to his physical body, a person may possess one or several 'astral bodies' which are in some way more rarified than the physical, or operate on a higher 'frequency of vibration'.

The facts of apparitional experiences as reported do not particularly favour the supposition that what is being seen is a spirit body of this kind. People do not only see more or less realistic human figures, but also a wide variety of partial or distorted representations of them. For example, the following are two cases in which the percipients report seeing the heads only of apparitional figures. In the first case, narrated by Prince Victor Duleep Singh, the head is 'framed' in a real picture in the subject's environment, and in the second it is seen as taking the place of the subject's own face reflected in a mirror:

Highclere Castle, Newbury, November 8th, 1894

On Saturday, October, 1893, I was in Berlin with Lord Carnarvon. We went to a theatre together and returned before midnight. I went to bed, leaving as I always do, a bright light in the room (electric light). As I lay in bed I found myself looking at an oleograph which hung on the wall opposite my bed. I saw distinctly the face of my father, the Maharajah Duleep Singh, looking at me, as it were out of this picture; not like a portrait of him, but his real head. The head about filled the picture frame. I continued looking and still saw my father looking at me with an intent expression. Though not in the least alarmed, I was so puzzled that I got out of bed to see what the picture really was. It was an oleograph common-place picture of a girl holding a rose and leaning out of a balcony, an arch forming a background. The girl's face was quite small, whereas my father's head was the size of life and filled the frame.

I was in no special anxiety about my father at the time, and had for some years known him to be seriously out of health; but there had been no news to alarm me about him.

Next morning (Sunday) I told the incident to Lord Carnarvon.

That evening (Sunday) late on returning home, Lord Carnarvon brought two telegrams into my room and handed them to me. I said at once, 'My father is dead.' That was the fact. He had had an apoplectic seizure on the Saturday evening at about nine o'clock, from which he never recovered, but continued unconscious and died on the Sunday, early in the afternoon. My father had often said to me that if I was not with him when he died he would try and come to me.

I am not subject to hallucinations, and have only once had any similar experience, when, as a schoolboy, I fancied I saw the figure of a dead schoolboy who had died in the room which I slept in with my brother; but I attach no importance to this.

VICTOR DULEEP SINGH

Lord Carnarvon writes:

I can confirm Prince V. Duleep Singh's account. I heard the incident from him on the Sunday morning. The same evening, at about 12 p.m., he received a telegram notifying him of his father's sudden illness and death. We had no knowledge of his father's illness. He has never told me of any similar previous occurrence.

CARNARVON

(*Journal of the S.P.R.*, Vol. VI, Dec. 1894, p. 368.)

Some years ago while brushing my hair before retiring, I was suddenly aware that the mirror appeared to distort, in the manner similar to the effect of a pebble tossed into water. The image of my face seemed to dissolve into the 'ripples' and then reform into the face of my father, not as I remembered him, a ruddy faced army major type, but as an old man, red rimmed eyes, with an expression of intense pain. I was naturally upset, and rushed into my sister's bed-room, insisting that something awful was going to happen to my mother. My sister and her husband insisted that it was imagination, but I was not convinced, and was quite sure that bad news in some form would be brought to us. The next morning, quite early, a tele-gram was brought to us saying that my brother was seriously ill with appendicitis in South Hants Hospital in Southampton. Now the strange fact is that my brother did not live in Southampton, he was merely in the district on business, and furthermore he was in the same hospital where 10 years previously my father had died of appendi-citis. Incidentally my sister told me later that the description I had given her of my father was in fact how he looked when he was dying. At that time I was too young to see him.

When people see apparitions of historical figures, these corres-pond more usually to an idea which they may have formed them-selves than to a precise representation of the historical figure in question as it actually was. For example, if someone had somehow acquired the erroneous idea that Nelson had blue eyes, and as a matter of historical fact he actually had brown ones, I should expect him to see an apparition of Nelson with blue eyes rather than brown ones. This is not, however, always the case. It is quite possible for an apparition to contain information which was not previously known to the subject. Even in these cases, however, there are indications that what we are dealing with is a hallucina-tion constructed to convey certain information. For example, in the following case, although the daughter was seen in a way which incorporated the information that she had been scratched, the figure which was seen did not correspond to any state of her physical body at any time, before or after death. The figure was seen with the colouring of a living person, but with a scratch which had not been made until after death. Since it was made after death, there was no time at which it had ever in reality been bright red, as it was seen on the apparition.

In 1867, my only sister, a young lady of 18 years, died suddenly of cholera, in St. Louis, Mo. My attachment for her was very strong, and the blow a severe one to me. A year or so after her death, the writer became a commercial traveller, and it was in 1876 while on one of my Western trips that the event occurred.

I had 'drummed' the city of St. Joseph, Mo., and had gone to my room at the Pacific House to send in my orders, which were unusually large ones, so that I was in a very happy frame of mind indeed. My thoughts, of course, were about these orders, knowing how pleased my house would be at my success. I had not been thinking of my late sister, or in any manner reflecting on the past. The hour was high noon, and the sun was shining cheerfully into my room. While busily smoking a cigar, and writing out my orders, I suddenly became conscious that some one was sitting on my left, with one arm resting on the table. Quick as a flash I turned and distinctly saw the form of my dead sister, and for a brief second or so looked her squarely in the face; and so sure was I that it was she, that I sprang forward in delight, calling her by name, and, as I did so, the apparition instantly vanished. Naturally I was startled and dumbfounded, almost doubting my senses; but the cigar in my mouth, and pen in hand, with the ink still moist on my letter, I satisfied myself I had not been dreaming and was wide awake. I was near enough to touch her, had it been a physical possibility, and noted her features, expression, and details of dress, etc. She appeared as if alive. Her eyes looked kindly and perfectly natural into mine. Her skin was so life-like that I could see the glow or moisture on its surface, and, on the whole, there was no change in her appearance, otherwise than when alive.

Now comes the most remarkable *confirmation* of my statement, which cannot be doubted by those who know what I state actually occurred. This visitation, or whatever you may call it, so impressed me that I took the next train home, and in the presence of my parents and others I related what had occurred. My father, a man of rare good sense and very practical, was inclined to ridicule me, as he saw how earnestly I believed what I stated; but he, too, was amazed when later on I told them of a bright red line or *scratch* on the right-hand side of my sister's face, which I distinctly had seen. When I mentioned this, my mother rose trembling to her feet and nearly fainted away, and as soon as she sufficiently recovered her self-possession, with tears streaming down her face, she exclaimed that I had indeed seen my sister, as no living mortal but herself was aware of that scratch, which she had accidentally made while doing some little act of kindness after my sister's death. She said she well remembered how pained she was to think she should have, unintentionally, marred the features of her dead daughter, and that unknown to all, how she had carefully obliterated all traces of the slight scratch with the aid of powder, etc., and that she had never mentioned it to a human being, from that day to this. In proof, neither my father nor any of our family had detected it, and positively were unaware of the incident, yet *I saw the scratch as bright as if just made*. So strangely impressed was my mother that even after she had retired to rest, she got up and dressed, came to me and told me *she knew* at least that I had seen my sister. A few weeks later my mother died, happy in her belief she would rejoin her favourite daughter in a better world.

In a further letter Mr. F. G. adds:

There was nothing of a spiritual or ghostly nature in either the form or dress of my sister, she appearing perfectly natural, and dressed in clothing that she usually wore in life, and which was familiar to me. From her position at the table, I could only see her *from the waist up*, and her appearance and everything she wore is indelibly photographed in my mind. I even had time to notice the collar and little breastpin she wore, as well as the comb in her hair, after the style then worn by young ladies. (*Proceedings of the S.P.R.*, Vol. VI, 1889–90, pp. 17–19.)

The percipient's father confirmed that his son had returned home and described the scratch on the apparition's face and that the percipient's mother had had to explain the significance of this feature to the percipient.

Of course, even if someone sees a figure of Nelson with eyes of the wrong colour, or a figure of a girl with a scratch which she did not have, it is quite possible for those who wish to do so to maintain that it was the surviving consciousness of Nelson or the girl, as the case may be, which deliberately stimulated the mind of the percipient to project this image. It is, of course, quite possible to suppose that when stimulated in such a way, the subconscious mind of the percipient may contribute some of its own prejudices and associations of ideas to the image which is projected. However, I cannot say that I find myself spending much time on such speculations—any more than I do on speculations that the human mind and nervous system may work exactly like a computer. Those who do, find such speculations of interest primarily because of their consistency with a system of belief about the nature of things.

What should concern us from a scientific point of view is those lines of investigation which are most capable of producing new data, and from this point of view it seems to me much preferable to concentrate attention on the mechanisms by which the human mind projects hallucinations of this kind, and the conditions under which it does so. This is what we have done in our study of apparitions (*Apparitions*, by Celia Green and Charles McCreery), and as they had never previously been studied with this in mind our work revealed several new aspects of the matter. However, this work requires to be carried further, and we are being prevented by inadequate finance from doing so.

*

It is curious that the human race has continued throughout the ages to learn so little about its own propensity for seeing hallucinations. This is shown by its remarkable unawareness of the phenomenon of out-of-the-body experiences, and also by its attitude to the seeing of hallucinations which has entered the general culture only as the derisive tradition of 'ghosts'. We have already discussed the illogical mental attitudes which are held towards these phenomena by those who know little or nothing about them. We shall now review the curiously selective and biased approach of those who have actually studied them.

As has already been mentioned, there is a tendency for pioneering advances in knowledge (that is, advances which the human race does not want made) to be viewed as very directly related to systems of belief. Consequently when the subject of apparitions has been studied, attention has been focused on whether they contributed to belief in extrasensory perception, or to belief in the survival of human personality after death. People were therefore most interested in studying cases in which the subject received information which he could not have obtained normally, particularly where this information was detailed, and the circumstances could be corroborated by other witnesses. Naturally, it was felt to be particularly interesting if the information obtained was of something which had been known only to a deceased person.

Perhaps the most celebrated case of this kind is the Chaffin Will case. A farmer in North Carolina, Mr. James A. Chaffin, had made a will in 1905 leaving his farm to the third of his four sons, Marshall, leaving his wife and his other three sons, James, John and Abner, unprovided for. In 1921 the father died and the third son, Marshall, duly took possession of his inheritance. However it appears that, unknown to anyone, the father had had remorse a few years before he died, as a result of reading the 27th chapter of Genesis, which tells of how Jacob supplanted his older brother Esau. He accordingly wrote out a second will in 1919, about two and a half years before he died, in which he divided his property equally between his four sons, and exhorted them: 'And if she is living, you all must take care of your mammy.' This second will the farmer hid in a manner shortly to be described.

The apparitional experiences which led to the finding of this will occurred to the second of Mr. Chaffin's four sons, James, i.e.

one of those excluded from the first will. He describes his experiences as follows:

> In all my life I never heard my father mention having made a later will than the one dated in 1905. I think it was in June of 1925 that I began to have very vivid dreams that my father appeared to me at my bedside but made no verbal communication. Some time later, I think it was the latter part of June, 1925, he appeared at my bedside again, dressed as I had often seen him dressed in life, wearing a black overcoat which I knew to be his own coat. This time my father's spirit spoke to me, he took hold of his overcoat this way and pulled it back and said, 'You will find my will in my overcoat pocket,' and then disappeared. The next morning I arose fully convinced that my father's spirit had visited me for the purpose of explaining some mistake. I went to mother's and sought for the overcoat but found that it was gone. Mother stated that she had given the overcoat to my brother John who lives in Yadkin County about twenty miles northwest of my home. I think it was on the 6th of July, which was on Monday following the events stated in the last paragraph I went to my brother's home in Yadkin County and found the coat. On examination of the inside pocket I found that the lining had been sewd together. I immediately cut the stitches and found a little roll of paper tied with a string which was in my father's handwriting and contained only the following words: 'Read the 27th chapter of Genesis in my daddie's old Bible.'
>
> At this point I was so convinced that the mystery was to be cleared up I was unwilling to go to mother's home to examine the old Bible without the presence of a witness and I induced a neighbour, Mr. Thos. Blackwelder to accompany me, also my daughter and Mr. Blackwelder's daughter were present. Arriving at mother's home we had a considerable search before we found the old Bible. At last we did find it in the top bureau drawer in an upstairs room. The book was so dilapidated that when we took it out it fell into three pieces. Mr. Blackwelder picked up the portion containing the Book of Genesis and turned the leaves until he came to the 27th chapter of Genesis and there we found two leaves folded together, the left hand page folded to the right and the right hand page folded to the left forming a pocket and in this pocket Mr. Blackwelder found the will which has been probated. [i.e. was probated in December, 1925.]
>
> During the month of December, 1925, my father again appeared to me about a week before the trial of the case of Chaffin *vs*. Chaffin and said 'Where is my old will,' and showed considerable temper. I believe from this that I would win the lawsuit as I did. I told my lawyer about this visitation the next morning. (*Proceedings of the S.P.R.*, Vol. 36, November 1927, pp. 519–20.)

It is not altogether clear from this account whether the percipient's experiences were typical apparitional experiences, in the sense of externalised hallucinations occurring during waking consciousness. A lawyer who questioned him reports that the percipient first said that he was awake, but on a 'rather rigid examination' admitted that he might have been in a 'doze'. However, the lawyer's 'rigid examination' did not necessarily lead to the most accurate statement of the situation. One observes that the percipient refers to his father appearing 'at my bedside', i.e. superimposed on his real environment, and this suggests a waking state, or possibly a false awakening, rather than a dream in the ordinary sense.

A case of this kind does not, of course, provide conclusive evidence of the survival of the deceased personality, since supposing extrasensory perception to exist, the information could always have been obtained by clairvoyance or possibly retrocognitively. In the case just quoted, for example, the following possibilities arise. The percipient could have obtained from his father by telepathy during the old man's lifetime the relevant information, which remained latent in his subconscious until pressure of circumstances caused it to surface in a dramatic form after the old man's death. Alternatively, the percipient could have become aware of the whereabouts of the will and of the message in the overcoat by extrasensory perception of the external world (such extrasensory perception is technically known as 'clairvoyance', to distinguish it from 'telepathy' which derives information from the mind of some other person). Or the percipient could have become aware by extrasensory perception of events which took place in the past (a process which is technically known as retrocognition). This retrocognition could have been either telepathic or clairvoyant in form—that is to say, it could have been retrocognition either of the sequence of actions formed by the old man in placing the will in the Bible and the message in the overcoat, or of the knowledge of this state of affairs that existed at a past time in the old man's mind.

The emphasis on the supposed importance of cases of a certain type led certainly to the collection of some striking evidence for the acquisition of information which could not have been normally obtained. But the evidence obtained in this form was shrugged off by the intellectual world as effortlessly as evidence of a similar quality for the existence of extrasensory perception occurring in other states. This approach also led to a relative unconcern, even on the part of the investigators themselves, with the conditions and mechanics of apparitional and hallucinatory experiences viewed purely as a perceptual phenomenon in their own right. It led also to a failure to perceive their relationship to other perceptual phenomena, such as lucid dreams and out-of-the-body experiences or even to common or garden hallucinations, and this situation continued until the study of apparitions made by this Institute.

At the back of everybody's mind, or at any rate at the back of too many minds, there seemed to be a preoccupation with showing apparitional phenomena to be something quite different from recognisable functions of the human nervous system, since the idea lurked that it was very desirable (or very undesirable) that an apparition should be shown to be 'really' the appearance in the physical world of a 'spirit' which possessed a 'spirit-body' and could locomote from our physical world to some more aethereal spirit-world.

Now, in fact, the seeing of apparitions of deceased persons cannot very well be viewed in isolation from the seeing of apparitions of people who are alive. The following is a case in point:

> My mother, two sisters and myself were living in Ramsgate. (My father was dead) and I was about 25 years old. My youngest sister brought home a girl to tea, she was a Catholic and we were C. of E. My mother, eldest sister and myself attended evening service at a small church nearby. The girl said she may come to church, following on. We were seated in a pew and the service was about to commence when I heard footsteps enter the church. Expecting Miss S. I looked round and saw her come in and walk across the aisle, apparently making her way towards us. I asked my mother to move up to make way for her to sit at the beginning of the pew. We made room, *I did not look round again*, but heard the footsteps cease about half-way down the aisle. I whispered to my mother that she probably had gone in another pew. After service, I hurried out and waited for her, but no Miss S., so I went home. My younger sister and her friend arrived home shortly afterwards. Attacked Miss S. and said I saw her come in church. *My sister* immediately replied, 'How could she? *She has been with me on the beach all evening.*'

The following is another case in which someone reports seeing an apparition of a living acquaintance for no very obvious reason:

> During a summer holiday in 1959 I was invited to supper with a friend who lived in Dorchester, Joan C. My husband and family returned to the village where we were staying and I walked along South Street, Dorchester, in the direction of Joan C.'s office. I had

arranged to call for her there just after 5 p.m. when she would finish her day's work.

I was a few minutes early, walking slowly. As I approached the building, I saw Joan C. coming towards me, pushing her bicycle. I was pleased that she had managed to leave early and quickened my pace. There were many people about but I could see her plainly, the distance between us decreasing. To my surprise she did not wave to me but turned to her left, as I thought into a small yard (there are several of these in South Street, where houses have been set back). I continued to walk on and turned to my right into the same yard.

To my amazement, not only was she not there, but there was no bicycle and no way in which she could have left the yard except by entering the house. I did not ring the bell but went on to her office. I enquired at the Reception if she had already left.

'Are you Mrs. Buckley?' the clerk asked—'Miss C. is waiting for you upstairs.'

I went up and found Joan C. in the clothes I had seen her wearing. I felt very cold all this time and could not tell her of the experience.

'I must fetch my bicycle' she said. It was in a yard at the back of the office.

As soon as one invites the public to send accounts of its hallucinatory experiences it becomes evident that it is quite a normal and a fairly common thing for sane people in good health to see, hear and otherwise experience a wide variety of things which are not there. Certainly the range of things which they perceive in this way includes the investigator's favourite kind of apparitional experience—that which fits best with the idea of a deceased person appearing to the living with something both meaningful and highly evidential to communicate. But this is relatively rare, and in addition people see apparitions of animals or objects, sometimes with an appearance of significance, but more often with no ascertainable rhyme or reason at all.

In the following case, for example, the percipient saw an apparition of a rabbit one night for no very obvious reason:

Some months after that, I had gone to bed and had slept for a couple of hours and had to get up to visit the bathroom. As I was about to leave the bedroom, the door of which opens inwards, I happened to see a fluffy white rabbit sitting at the foot of the door. I stood there for a couple of seconds to make sure of what I was seeing. I then bent down in attempt to touch the back of the rabbit and it disappeared. I even found myself turning the light on and running my hand over the carpet where the rabbit had been sitting.

So far as we, and previous investigators, can observe, the

subjects who report these hallucinatory experiences are otherwise perfectly normal, and have no more psychiatric history than the population at large. However, it is again a pity that the issue of whether or not it is only the mentally deranged who see apparitions and hallucinations has been regarded as so momentous and emotionally loaded. It frequently seems to be implied that if apparitions are seen only by persons with some classifiable or ascertainable form of mental illness, we should be quite justified in disregarding the phenomenon. In fact, it is also (even if implicitly) held that science at large is justified in ignoring the phenomenon unless and until it can be rigorously demonstrated that all the persons who see apparitions qualify as sane and normal.

To demonstrate this rigorously is, indeed, impossible by virtue of the total uncertainty, to which reference is so frequently made in rejecting the findings of investigations in this field. It would be possible, granted a very considerable sum of money, to produce a demonstration more elaborate than any which has yet been attempted, by interviewing and submitting to lengthy questionnaires every single individual who reported an apparition or a hallucination. Elaborate and costly though this would be, there is no reason why the findings should carry conviction with those who wish to remain unconvinced.

In fact, while after eighteen years in the subject I have a strong impression that those who see apparitions do not differ from the normal population, and that the few mentally ill people who do respond to appeals are at once identifiable as such, I cannot say that this has ever seemed to me a very important issue. Even if it were the case that these phenomena were produced by the human nervous system only in conditions of mental illness, they would still be remarkable phenomena, and worthy of investigation as such.

It would, it seems to me, be more interesting if both hallucinations of the sane and hallucinations of the insane were to be studied as phenomena which shed some light on the workings of the human perceptual mechanism, and if any parallels which may exist between the two classes were regarded as potentially informative, as well as any differences. (Such a study is only likely to be made by this Institute, if at all.) However, in fact neither class has been studied to any extent as objectively interesting in this way, let alone in relation to each other. For example, the most informative

account of the hallucinations of the insane is still that given by
Bleuler in his book on schizophrenia, first published over sixty
years ago.[1]

Although it is accepted that it is characteristic of certain forms
of insanity for hallucinations to occur, there has been no systematic attempt to find out more about them than that. It is, incidentally, curious to note that people are prepared to accept that
the insane do have hallucinations. If they were as suspicious as they
are towards hallucinations reported by sane people, they might
well have come to the conclusion that it was typical for insane
people to tell lies of certain characteristic kinds, but that nobody
ever saw or heard anything which was not there.

In fact, it is evidently felt to be quite suitable that hallucinations
should be characterised as things which happen to the insane, this
being viewed as sufficient reason for regarding them as a dis-
credited phenomenon, about which nothing further need be known.
There is also a curious belief that when an apparition is reported it
is relevant to discuss at great length the precise degree of normality
and social adjustment of the percipient, apparently in relation to a
belief that the phenomenon can in some curious way be 'rejected'
if the percipient's record of mental stability is less than admirable.

In fact, when apparitions are studied as phenomena in their own
right, the most obvious thing which emerges is that the human
nervous system appears to have a remarkable facility for projecting
complete reproduction environments. Now this is a matter well
worthy of study and attention by all those with any interest in
theories of sensory perception. However, it is clearly unlikely to be
accorded this attention since it does not immediately contribute to
the confirmation of standard dogma. The standard dogmatic belief
on the matter, although necessarily vague as there is little precise
observation which supports it, is that sensory perception is produced in an entirely mechanical fashion as a result of afferent
impulses from the various sensory organs, caused by the interaction of the human body with the physical world.

The occurrence of *metachoric experiences* is difficult to square
with this belief.

A metachoric experience is defined as one in which the subject's
normal environment is completely replaced by a hallucinatory one,

[1] Eugen Bleuler, *Dementia Praecox or the Group of Schizophrenias*,
International Universities Press, New York, 1950.

and we know that metachoric experiences of several different types have been reported. In some the new, hallucinatory environment bears little or no relationship to the percipient's real environment at the time. Thus in a lucid dream the subject seldom dreams that he is in his own bedroom. However, in other metachoric experiences the subject's real environment is replaced by an almost identical replica, as in the majority of involuntary or spontaneous out-of-the-body experiences, in which the subject usually finds himself looking at the same scene as just before the experience, only from a different point of view.

Yet another kind of metachoric experience is the 'false awakening', in which the dreamer seems to wake from a lucid, or occasionally a non-lucid, dream only to realise subsequently that this 'awakening' was only part of his dream. The place in which he seems to wake may be an apparently exact hallucinatory replica of his real environment at the time, that is, his own bedroom, or it may be a representation of some other place, such as a bedroom in which he used to sleep but does no longer. The following are two examples of false awakenings in which lucid dreamers seemed to 'wake up' in their true environments at the time:

> Yesterday morning I was dreaming and knew I was dreaming because I could walk on the wall, and the door frame was crooked. Anyway, after dreaming awhile I remembered reading in your book that if one says their own name in a dream, that they will wake up. Consequently I said my first name three times and slowly started to wake up. I was a little dizzy because I stood up too fast, and had trouble walking because my 'foot was asleep' (common expression for pressure on nerves from lying on arms or legs wrong). I knew I was no longer dreaming because I could no longer walk on the wall and the door frame was straight. I went to the front door and found a note saying that the police would return some stolen goods that afternoon. (There had been some prowlers in the neighbourhood the past week.) The note was very sloppy and had poor grammar. I went into the bedroom and found the stolen items were still there, and much to my surprise, I awoke. It took another minute to straighten things out in my mind.

> Seemed to wake; X entered the room, switched on electric light and drew curtains to exclude sunlight. (I had been sleeping late, so it was in fact late morning.) This appeared natural but of course should have seemed illogical. I told X of the lucid dream I had just been having, and thought of the possibility that this was still a dream. I believe I even discussed this with X, but dismissed it because of the

naturalness of everything. I went over to the window and noted the detail of everything—papers spread out on the carpet under the window, spotted with rain that had come in through it. (In actual fact, I did not at this time have any papers spread out in this way—I don't think I ever did while I lived there.) I believe I remember thinking that it could not be a dream, because it could not so accurately reproduce so much detail—looking at the numerous papers, feeling their texture, thickness, etc., as I thought this.

Some, or even all, apparitional experiences are also metachoric. For example, in the following case the percipient reports seeing an apparition of a deceased person with her eyes closed, so clearly not only is the figure of the apparition hallucinatory but the rest of the scene before her as well:

My dear friend had recently died, quite suddenly, leaving a widow (Alice) and five young children. Two days after his death I went out and sat in the garden, where he had helped me work some time previously. I was extremely distressed, this being my first experience of the loss of a close friend. In my distress, I sat down, closed my eyes (wanting not to cry) and said, 'Oh, Mac—if I knew you were all right, I wouldn't feel so bad.' Then I 'saw' him standing in front of me, though my eyes were closed—I could see him, the garden, everything just as though my eyes were open, tho' perhaps a bit less bright (it was a very sunny day). He smiled at me and said, 'It's great to be free.' This was quite consistent with his usual manner of speech. I said, 'But what about Alice and the children—how will she manage?' and he said, 'Alice is a good kid, she'll be okay.' Then I said, 'Are you really all right?' and reached out to touch him, opening my eyes at the same time. I seemed to feel his touch on my hand, but he was gone. I felt completely comforted, as his whole appearance and speech were completely typical of what I had often experienced in normal conversations with him.

Once the concept of metachoric experiences has been formulated, it is clearly of relevance in relation to hallucinations which occur in illness. It may be that there are two distinct types of hallucination, those which are and those which are not metachoric, but the phenomena have not yet been studied with this in mind. However, there is one class of hallucinations which occur in illness which clearly suggest that they may well be metachoric. Some of the hallucinations which occur at the onset of epileptic attacks are very curious, in that elaborate and seemingly realistic objects appear integrated with the normal environment. Thus, one subject used to see a line of miniature red buses running across the floor, and another subject used to both see and hear a witch-woman rattling the utensils in her kitchen.

*

Now it may well be asked why there should be such an aversion to the study of apparitions and other forms of hallucinatory experience as phenomena. They do not appear in a very direct manner to contradict the mechanical computer belief about the nervous system. In fact, it would be difficult for them to do so, as this has never been worked out with sufficient completeness. Certainly it would not appear that the study of hallucinatory states would make it impossible for anyone who wished to do so to believe that the brain worked in a mechanical computer-like way.

However, the study of metachoric experiences inevitably throws a certain doubt on the status of our perceptions of the external world.

This is bound to suggest the idea that the environment we perceive is something which is constructed and projected to express both information which is derived by physiological means from the physical world, and also more psychologically determined elements, which may at times include information obtained by extrasensory perception. Since what most people perceive most of the time is based entirely on information derived from the physical world, and since this is used in the construction of a hallucinatory environment according to more or less constant laws, the perceptual environment is believed to be an automatic and mechanical result of afferent impulses.

A further possibility which suggests itself is that all perception is actually of a kind which we now call extrasensory perception, but that most people's experience most of the time contains only that selection of perceptions about the external world which are compatible with the belief that there is an external physical world, which they, in common with other people, are perceiving according to certain physical laws.

I am not, of course, suggesting this as an alternative dogmatic belief, nor do I think it would be at all profitable for people to engage in discussion about which belief they find the nicer to believe. However, this speculative hypothesis is certainly among the thoughts which are evoked by a consideration of the phenomena, and it seems to me in no way objective or scientific to reject it from consideration.

Further, it may actually be profitable to be aware that it is people's aversion to entertaining ideas of this kind which makes them so extremely uninterested in making a thorough scientific study of any phenomena which might force them on their attention.

CHAPTER 14

Psychokinesis

PSYCHOKINESIS, or the seeming influence of mind over matter, is even less compatible with people's dogmatic beliefs than is telepathy or lucid dreaming. It is difficult at first sight to see why this should be so, since none of them are compatible with the beliefs of modern science. However, I have heard people who were convinced of the existence of telepathy declaring that, while it seemed to them quite acceptable that mind should interact with mind, they just felt it could not be right for mind to interact with matter. In saying this, they were very likely making explicit an emotional prejudice which has inhibited the investigation of psychokinesis. The belief system which appears to be implied is one in which the reality of the physical world is unquestionably accepted, but in which it is supposed that human beings may have a spiritual component. It is, on this view, even found emotionally appealing that human beings should interact with one another by telepathy as well as indirectly by means of the physical world. This underlines the alleged importance of human beings to other human beings, and may be taken as supporting the anthropocentric outlook so beloved of the human race.

To give the reader some idea of the sort of phenomenon which is in question, let us pause to give some examples.

Several people have independently reported to us that on one or more occasions as children they descended the stairs without touching the steps. The following is a case of this kind.

> When I was about 7 or 8 years old (I am now 66) I was going downstairs one afternoon. The staircase was a typical one, divided into two short flights. As I started to descend the second flight I stepped off the top stair and floated to the ground. I can feel the sensation now.

My father was a writer, and was working at home in his study. I called out to him in excitement, and he came out of the room to see what was the matter. I told him that I had 'flown' downstairs. He was a very unusual man, and he believed me, and questioned me about it. Shortly after this we moved to another house, and my experience was never repeated.

I certainly did not *try* to do it, because such an idea had never entered my mind. It just happened, and as I stepped off the top stair I felt myself floating downwards. It was a very pleasant sensation, I can remember that. I felt very light.

The following is a similar example of apparent psychokinesis, spontaneously reported to us. In this instance the subject reports not just one 'levitation', as in the first case, but several.

When I was about eight years of age, I, one day, suddenly realised that for some time past (I don't remember for how long) I had literally been 'flying' down the staircase at my home. As far as I remember, I took a tiny little flip into the air at the top of the stair-case, and more-or-less floated down, landing gently on the mat at the bottom of it, without my feet touching any part of the stairs on the way. I also remember that on the day I became conscious of this, I immediately lost the 'art'.

Of course, as there were no witnesses in these two cases, it is possible that they were both examples of unidentified out-of-the-body experiences; that is, the percipient's body may really have been walking down the stairs in the normal way, while his consciousness seemed to be observing the scene from a different vantage point. In the majority of out-of-the-body experiences, the percipient seems to see his own body from the outside. In the cases we have quoted one might suppose that the subconscious mind of the percipient chose instead to construct the hallucinatory scene without including a representation of the percipient's body descending the stairs.

However, while pointing out that these cases may have been unidentified out-of-the-body experiences, we should not lose sight of the fact that they may not have been, since a number of cases are on record in which witnesses have corroborated that a levitation actually occurred.

The following is a report of a 'levitation' of a rather different kind for which the ecsomatic explanation seems *prima facie* to be excluded, since the inexplicable movement of the subject's body was apparently witnessed by a number of other people:

My only experience of levitation occurred during a lunch-time break at school, when I was seventeen years of age.

The whole experiment was regarded as rather a joke by the members of the class who participated in it—none of us really expecting anything extraordinary to happen at all.

Each girl took her turn lying on a long wooden table at the front of the classroom, with the others gathered *tightly* around her, so that there were no gaps. I remember thinking as I lay on the table, that the effect of the dark uniforms shutting off the light made it seem very shaded and cocoon-like. As one lay there the girls chanted a rhyme—the actual words of which I have forgotten, but which referred to the person on the table as looking white, ill and then dead. It was spoken quite slowly and in unison so that its drone-like tone had great depth and was very penetrating.

Several girls took part before me, but without much success. Some had not risen at all from the table and were quite disillusioned, convinced that our initial scepticism had been confirmed. Others however did admit to feeling a strange sensation which they found inexplicable and it was this plus the declaration of a friend that she had felt a slight levitation which encouraged me to try it.

I have absolutely no explanation why I was able to rise approximately three feet from the table surface. I was perfectly conscious that I was rising and might even have uttered an exclamation of surprise in response to the great upheaval the event had caused amongst the girls. The rapidity of the rise and indeed the fact that I had risen at all caused me to jerk my body out of the lying position and with much commotion the girls cushioned my fall.

The following is another case in which there were apparently witnesses for the levitation which was reported. The narrator is E. A. Smythies, C.I.E., then British Forestry Adviser to the Government of Nepal. The incident occurred in Kathmandu in 1941, and the following account is based on contemporary notes:

Before I describe the actual incident, some preliminary remarks are necessary. I was told that some Nepalis have to do periodic *puja* or sacrifice to their *Bhagwan* or spirit at their home village. If they fail to do this at the right time, the *Bhagwan* comes, wherever they may be, and possesses them. They lose consciousness, dance and shout and behave madly while under control. . . .

A month or two later we had a little dinner party, and after dinner about nine p.m. we were sitting in the dark in the drawing-room admiring a film of big game shooting in Nepal kindly sent by H.H. the Maharaja, when Azmat came quietly into the room and whispered in my ear, 'Bhagwan phir a gaya,' i.e. 'Bhagwan has come again'. I did not want to disturb the party, so I slipped out quietly and went to the back of the house, where the servants' quarters were. These quarters were a building of brick and tiled roof divided into five

rooms in a row, each room about ten feet by seven and eight feet
high, with a small extension at the back for cooking food, and a door
three and a half by six feet high in front, and well lit with an un-
shaded electric light bulb. In one of these little bare rooms—there
was nothing in the room except a roll of bedding in one corner and
a small box in another—my elder orderly, aged about twenty-two
and also called Krishna, was squatting quite alone on the bare floor,
dressed in a shirt and khaki shorts with bare legs. His attitude was
approximately as shown in the accompanying illustration [not re-
produced here], cross-legged with his hands clasped between his
legs. His head and body were shaking and quivering, his face appeared wet with sweat, and he was making the most extraordinary
noises. He seemed to me obviously unconscious of what he was doing
or that a circle of rather frightened servants—and myself—were
looking at him through the open door at about eight or ten feet
distance.

This went on for about ten minutes or a quarter of an hour, when
suddenly (with his legs still crossed and his hands clasped) he rose
about two feet in the air, and after about a second bumped down
hard on the floor. This happened again twice, exactly the same except
that his hands and legs became separated.

One of the servants whispered that the *Bhagwan* was very angry
with Krishna and was punishing him by bumping him on the floor in
this way, which, I must admit, was just what it looked like. The
servants were becoming very frightened and worried, and I was
feeling very creepy myself at this inexplicable sight. Then one of the
Nepali servants produced a splinter of resinous wood, which he lit
and placed the burning end in Krishna's mouth for a moment. The
seizure continued unaltered for a brief interval, and then suddenly
it passed, and Krishna opened his eyes and relaxed. He sat looking
dazed but otherwise normal. Shortly afterwards I left and returned
to our party, from which I had been absent for less than half an hour.

That is a detailed description of what I saw, and noted down the
next morning. I cannot explain it.

To touch on one or two more points:

(1) I am quite convinced there was no fake; the whole thing was
unpremeditated and unexpected, with the orderly an unwilling, or
rather unconscious, medium of an extraordinary manifestation.

(2) There was no possibility of any apparatus, such as a thin wire,
having been rigged up to haul the man up and down. There was an
excellent light, and I was quite close, and could see the whole of the
small room. Nor could he have been pushed up from below, since he
was sitting on a bare solid brick floor. When the levitation took place,
the seven or eight other spectators, who were all my servants, were
outside the room with me, and could not have 'assisted' in any way.

(3) I was not in the least under the influence of alcohol (my limit is
one 'chota peg'), and nor were the servants around me, who saw
what I saw.

(4) It is, I think, an impossibility for anyone to *jump* from the position shown in Figure I to that in Figure II. At any rate I have tried it myself and cannot move an inch from the ground. (*Journal of the S.P.R.*, Vol. 36, 1951, pp. 415–17.)

The following points were brought out by the editor of the Journal in which the above account appeared; they are based on further information supplied by Mr. Smythies.

(2) Mr. Smythies was not prepared for levitation to take place—'I was certainly *not*', he writes, 'expecting anything like levitation'; (3) the height of about two feet to which the elder Krishna was levitated 'was a sort of average, his feet a few inches lower, his seat about three feet up. That is the impression I have'; (4) Krishna did not immediately drop to the ground after each levitation—'I had the impression of one or two seconds pause at the top—not more.' (*Ibid.*, pp. 418–19.)

The cases we have quoted are not selected on grounds of evidential value, but they illustrate some of the types of psychokinesis which are reported as occurring relatively spontaneously, and incidentally suggest that such phenomena may happen more commonly than is generally realised.[1]

As I have already pointed out, the human race shows distinct signs of emotional disturbance in connection with the idea that the external world *in toto* may be illusory. However, if this were considered as a hypothesis, it would be clear that psychokinesis would scarcely seem too outrageous a phenomenon. (Though, personally, I do not see that it is so outrageous even on the real-physical-world hypothesis. If mind does interact with matter that is simply the way things are, and we had better find out about it.)

If the world of our perceptions is illusory, and everyone is merely colluding in perceiving a world which seems to operate according to certain definite physical laws, we might suppose that occasionally groups of people broke the rules, and perceived physical objects behaving in ways which did not agree with the social conventions.

*

[1] The evidential value of some cases is discussed by my colleague Charles McCreery in his book *Science, Philosophy and ESP*, Chapters 4–6.

The evidence for psychokinesis, when it occurs, is of course shrugged aside in the same way as evidence for extrasensory perception. However, it would appear that the emotional resistance to the idea of psychokinesis is more profound, so the resistance to its entering the general culture has been even greater. It is not too difficult to encounter educated people who have a dim idea that research (although of course they do not know what) has been carried out on telepathy to such a point that it is reasonable to sound as though one accepts the phenomenon, but it is much rarer to encounter anyone with a similar outlook towards psychokinesis. The emotional resistance to psychokinesis in human psychology also has the effect that fewer people can be found to do it successfully, and these few usually have to expend some effort in entering some kind of trance or other specialised state of consciousness.

One of the outstanding subjects of the past, an Italian woman called Eusapia Palladino, exhibited various degrees or levels of trance during the production of her phenomena. These have been described by one investigator, the Hon. Everard Fielding, as follows:

> Her own condition varied greatly. She exhibited three stages of consciousness. During the continuance of the brighter light in which the séance generally opened she remained perfectly normal, and it was in this state as a rule that the levitations of the séance table, which will be later described, took place. She would then gradually sink into a condition of half-trance, preluded as a rule by numerous yawns and amazing hiccoughs. In this state she still speaks and answers questions, though her manner is quieter than in her normal state, her speech oppressed and plaintive, and her eyes clouded. She professes to have no recollection of events that take place in this state.
>
> . . . Of her third state, that of deep trance, we did not have many examples. It was, however, generally coincident with the more complex phenomena. *Ex hypothesi*, while in this state she is under the complete influence of her 'control', 'John King'. She speaks sometimes in a deep voice, refers to herself in the third person as 'my daughter' or 'the medium', and addresses the sitters as 'thou'. She laughs occasionally in a raucous, almost diabolic manner, and her expression is at times fierce and forbidding. But as a rule she is apparently overwhelmed by sleep, throws herself often into the arms of her neighbours, remains entirely passive, and surrenders herself completely to their control. (*Proceedings of the S.P.R.*, Vol. 23, 1908, pp. 324-5.)

We shall give just one example of an ostensibly psychokinetic phenomenon produced by this subject. Her depth of trance on this particular occasion is not mentioned, but the fact that she and the experimenters were standing up at the time suggests that she was not in the deepest stage. The incident took place at a series of experiments on the Ile Roubaud, a small island in the Mediterranean belonging to Professor Charles Richet, the physiologist. The three experimenters were Richet himself, the physicist Sir Oliver Lodge, and F. W. H. Myers. The reader must imagine that the experimenters and the subject are standing round a small table in the sitting room of Professor Richet's house, with Myers holding Palladino on one side, and Richet on the other, while Lodge held the free hands of the other two experimenters. The following is Myers' account of the incident. (The notes he refers to were dictated while the phenomena were going on to Dr. Julian Ochorowicz, a lecturer in psychology at the University of Warsaw, sitting outside the window of the experimental room.)

It so happened that I received the most violent of the pressures experienced at these sittings, and also the only pressure, I think, felt at three separate points at once. In the notes for July 26th occur the words: 'M. was seized from behind as by a bear and compressed. It turned him about and ultimately drew him violently away from L., who saw him moving, and felt the transmitted pull. M. then felt as if a big man were kneeling behind him seizing him round back and thighs, and shaking him vigorously. Embrace strong and lasting.' Here, when I say 'seized round back and thighs', I mean that the feeling was as if a powerful head were butting me in the small of the back, while I was shaken sideways, first to one side then to the other, by something which pressed strongly on both hips, though without, in this case, any definite sensation of *fingers*. When I say 'as by a bear' I mean that the grip was stiff and massive rather than flexible, as opposed to cases where apparent palm and finger-tips were felt. There were, at any rate, strong simultaneous pressures on three different regions of my body, and with a force which impressed me at the time as being greater than my own. I was holding the hands of Professor Lodge and of Eusapia; Professor Richet, the only other person in the room, was holding the other hands of Professor Lodge and Eusapia, and we were all standing round the table. Professor Ochorowicz was outside the window, taking notes, and no one else could possibly have been present. (*Journal of the S.P.R.*, Vol. VI, 1894, p. 337.)

An interesting point about this occurrence is that Myers was standing so close in front of a buffet that a person would apparently not have been able to get behind him to produce the effects normally even had one been there to do so. This emerges from a note Myers wrote later about the same incident, in response to the suggestion that Eusapia might have produced the touches normally:

> We were at this time (12.50) standing round the small table in close proximity. There was quite enough light to enable me to see her whole figure well,—as is shown by the fact the just preceding entry in the notes relates to an object seen by all of us. I held Eusapia's hand, and was also more or less in contact all the time with her dress and person, owing to our standing so close together. Between me and the *buffet* behind me was a space (as we afterwards computed) of a few inches only; in fact I was standing just clear of it. (*Ibid.*, Vol. VII, 1895, p. 62.)

An apparent exception to the rule that most psychokinesis subjects need to enter a dissociated state for producing their phenomena was Daniel Dunglas Home. He certainly had a light trance state, but many of his phenomena were produced when he was not in it. Sir William Crookes, the physicist, who carried out a number of experiments on Home's phenomena during the 1870s made the following comment at the time of the Ile Roubaut experiments with Eusapia Palladino:

> In the first place, most if not all the occurrences with Eusapia seem to have taken place when she was in a trance, and the more complete the trance the more striking the phenomena. This was not always so with Home. Certainly the two most striking things I ever saw with him, the fire test and visible forms, were to be observed while he was entranced, but it was not easy to tell when he was in that state, for he spoke and moved about almost as if he were in his normal condition; the chief differences being that his actions were more deliberate, and his manner and expressions more solemn, and he always spoke of himself in the third person, as 'Dan'. (*Ibid.*, Vol. VI, 1894, p. 341.)

However, Home always protested that the phenomena that occurred in his presence were in no way his doing, but the work of 'the spirits'. He thus evaded direct responsibility for what was going on.

Sir William Crookes has left an interesting account of the apparent levitations he witnessed in Home's presence:

> The best cases of Home's levitation I witnessed were in my own house. On one occasion he went to a clear part of the room, and after standing quietly for a minute, told us he was rising. I saw him slowly rise up with a continuous gliding movement and remain about six

inches off the ground for several seconds, when he slowly descended. On this occasion no one moved from their places. On another occasion I was invited to come to him, when he rose 18 inches off the ground, and I passed my hands under his feet, round him, and over his head when he was in the air.

On several occasions Home and the chair on which he was sitting at the table rose off the ground. This was generally done very deliberately, and Home sometimes then tucked up his feet on the seat of the chair and held up his hands in view of all of us. On such an occasion I have got down and seen and felt that all four legs were off the ground at the same time, Home's feet being on the chair. Less frequently the levitating power extended to those sitting next to him. Once my wife was thus raised off the ground in her chair. (*Journal of the S.P.R.*, Vol VI, 1894, pp. 341–2.)

The emotional resistance to the idea of mind directly influencing matter is scarcely reasonable. We know little enough about the essential nature of either; if it should be found that they interact, then that is a fact about them. I do not really see why the human race should have this vested interest in believing that they do not interact in this way. After all, it is difficult to escape from the fact that they interact in some way, about which we still know very little, although most people evidently find this undisturbing so long as the influence of the individual's mind over matter does not extend beyond the surface of the individual's skin. Hume contrived to be more aware than most people that the nature of the interaction, even within the body, presented a fundamental problem:

> The motion of our body follows upon the command of our will. Of this we are every moment conscious. But the means, by which this is effected; the energy, by which the will performs so extraordinary an operation; of this we are so far from being immediately conscious, that it must for ever escape our most diligent enquiry. . . .
>
> Were we empowered, by a secret wish, to remove mountains, or control the planets in their orbit; this extensive authority would not be more extraordinary, nor more beyond our comprehension. (*An Enquiry Concerning Human Understanding*, Section VII, Part I, quoted in *The Empiricists*, pp. 352–3.)[1]

People may perhaps be under the impression that the situation has been fundamentally altered by the staggering progress made

---

[1] For a further discussion of the philosophical problems raised by both psychokinesis and ordinary movement see Chapter 5 of *Psychical Phenomena and the Physical World* by Charles McCreery.

in physiological research since the days of Hume, but in fact this is far from being so. Attempts to give an account in physical terms of the functioning of the nervous system are very incomplete (although I do not mean to suggest that I have a dogmatic belief that they could never be made more complete—in this field, as in most others, research has been sporadic and uncoordinated). Such account as can be given of the functioning of the nervous system falls far short of accounting for the relationship between mental events and physiological processes.

There is, I think, a general presumption, at least among the leaders of fashionable thought, that the correlation between physical events in the nervous system and mental events can, in principle and at some future date, be shown to be so precise that we shall be justified in discarding consciousness as an epiphenomenon of physiology. This assumption may be detected in, among other things, those brightly *avant-garde* suggestions that the correct approach to the study of human happiness is by way of neurophysiology or biochemistry. It does not appear to me that, however precise the correlation between physical and mental events might in the future become, one could ever escape from the fact that one is discussing a correlation of two different things.

Curiously enough, there is another context in which modern thought wishes to discard a phenomenon as not 'real', on the grounds that it is totally defined by another phenomenon. In theoretical physics it is found convenient, in considerations of parity, to treat the magnetic field as having no right to be treated as possessing physical reality, since it is completely determined by the movements of electric charges.

In the study of psychokinesis, even more than in that of phenomena such as metachoric experiences which may to a certain extent be studied from a purely psychological point of view, the absurdity of attempting to proceed without the most elaborate laboratory facilities is immediately apparent. Until the physical and physiological conditions of the phenomena are studied and placed on an objective basis, the present situation will continue. This situation is that, however minute the attention to evidential considerations may be in any particular experiment, it will always be possible for those motivated to do so to regard it as subjective and liable to error and misinterpretation of various kinds—in any event, as providing no reason why money for the further study of psychokinesis should be placed in the hands of anyone motivated to make such a study. In ignoring the evidence for psychokinesis, as in ignoring that for extrasensory perception, the sceptics are always greatly assisted by the passage of time. Once any particular piece of evidence has been reported it is only necessary to start ignoring it. In due course, the people who were concerned in making the observations become old and die. Even before this happens, the lapse of five or ten years goes far to rob an experiment of immediacy and definition in everyone's mind; it is already much easier to generate an aura of vagueness and uncertainty about what actually happened.

There can be no solution to this situation in the pursuit of further pieces of evidence on the same terms as those which have already been ignored. The ostensible pursuit of such evidence by persons who are socially accredited scientists in other fields, but who have not seen fit to devote their lives to parapsychology, is particularly suspect. Usually they do not even take the trouble to acquaint themselves with the work of the early psychical researchers.

CHAPTER 15

Precognition

PEOPLE commonly raise the question whether what is perceived in precognitive, and indeed in retrocognitive, cases is the future or the past as it 'really will be' or 'really was', or whether it is a kind of symbolic representation which contains some correct elements. Naturally the types of case which most impress people are those in which the precognitive perception offers the most complete and detailed correspondence with the future event to which it corresponds.

The following is an example of an ostensibly precognitive dream in which an impressive number of details about an event six years in the future were represented in an apparently realistic way. The percipient, whose account follows, is described as 'Lady Q'.

> I have been asked to give an account of an experience which was certainly the most remarkable in my life :- a dream which came to me three times at long intervals, and which was at last fulfilled.
>
> My father died when I was a child; my mother married again, and I went to live with an uncle, who became like a father to me. In the spring of 1882 I dreamt that my sister and I were sitting in my uncle's drawing-room. In my dream it was a brilliant spring day, and from the window we saw quantities of flowers in the garden, many more than were in fact to be seen from that window. But over the garden there lay a thin covering of snow. I knew in my dream that my uncle had been found dead by the side of a certain bridle-path about three miles from the house—a field-road where I had often ridden with him, and along which he often rode when going to fish in a neighbouring lake. I knew that his horse was standing by him, and that he was wearing a dark homespun suit of cloth made from the wool of a herd of black sheep which he kept. I knew that his body was being brought home in a waggon with two horses, with hay in the bottom, and that we were waiting for his body to arrive. Then in my dream the waggon came to the door; and two men well known to me—one a gardener, the other the kennel huntsman—

helped to carry the body up the stairs, which were rather narrow. My uncle was a very tall and heavy man, and in my dream I saw the men carrying him with difficulty, and his left hand hanging down and striking against the banisters as the men mounted the stairs. This detail gave me in my dream an unreasonable horror. I could not help painfully thinking, Oh, why did they not prevent his hand from being bruised in this way?

In the sadness and horror of this sight I awoke, and I slept no more that night. I had determined not to tell my uncle of the dream; but in the morning I looked so changed and ill that I could not escape his affectionate questioning; and at last I told him of my vision of him lying dead in that field-road. I had no anxiety about his health. He was a robust man of sixty-six, accustomed to hunt his own pack of hounds and to take much exercise. He listened to me very kindly, and although he was not himself at all alarmed by my dream, he offered me to do anything I liked which might calm my mind. I begged him to promise me never to go alone by that particular road. He promised me that he would always make an excuse to have a groom or some one with him; I remember my compunction at the thought of giving him this trouble—and yet I could not help asking for his promise.

The impression of the dream grew gradually fainter, but it did not leave me; and I remember that when a little boy came to stay with us some time after, and boy-like drew his stick along the banisters as he went upstairs, the sound brought back the horror of my dream. Two years passed by, and the thought of the dream was becoming less frequent, when I dreamt it again with all its details the same as before, and again with the same profoundly disturbing effect. I told my uncle, and said to him that I felt sure that he had been neglecting his promise, and riding by that field-road alone. He admitted that he had occasionally done so, 'although,' he said, 'I think I have been very good on the whole.' He renewed the promise; and again the impression grew weaker as four years passed by, during which I married and left his home. In the May of 1888 I was in London, expecting my baby. On the night before I was taken ill, I dreamt the same dream again, but with this variation. Instead of dreaming that I was at my uncle's home with my sister, I knew in my dream that I was lying in bed in our London house. But from that bedroom, just as from the drawing-room in the former dreams, I seemed to see my uncle lying dead in the same well-known place. And I seemed also to perceive the same scene of the bringing home of the body. Then came a new point. As I lay in bed, a gentleman dressed in black, but whose face I could not see, seemed to stand by me and tell me that my uncle was dead. I woke in great distress. But as I was ill from then for two days, as soon as the child was born I ceased to dwell on the dream—only I felt an overpowering desire to write at once to my uncle myself and to tell him that I was getting better. I was not allowed to do this; but afterwards I managed to write a few lines in pencil unknown to any one but the nurse. This note reached my uncle two days before his death.

As I grew better, I began to wonder greatly at not hearing from my uncle, who generally wrote to me every day. Then my dream came back to me, and I was certain that he was ill or dead—but my husband, nurse, and maid (all I saw) seemed cheerful as usual. Then one morning my husband said my step-father wished to see me, and I at once guessed his errand. He entered the room dressed in black and stood by my bedside. At once I recognised that this was the figure which I had seen in my dream. I said, 'The Colonel is dead— I know all about it—I have dreamt it often.' And as he was unable to speak from emotion, I told him all about it, place, time of day (morning), and the clothes my uncle wore.

Then I thought of that scene on the staircase, which had always remained in my mind. I asked if there were any bruises on the hands. 'No bruises,' said my step-father, 'either on hands or face.' He thought that I fancied that my uncle had fallen from his horse. Soon afterwards my sister—the sister who had been in my dream—came to see me, and brought me a ring which my uncle had always worn on his left hand. I was very thankful for this memento of him; and I told my sister how I had feared that the ring would have been forgotten. 'I only came just in time,' she said; 'they were just going to close the coffin.' 'Was there any bruise on the left hand?' I asked. At first she said that there was not; but then she said she thought there was a bluish discoloration across the back of the first joints of the fingers. She did not know how it had been caused. When I was well enough to travel, I went to my old home; there I saw my old nurse, who had been in the house when my uncle died. Her account, added to my stepfather's enabled me to realise the events of that day. My uncle had received my pencil note on the Sunday morning, and had been greatly pleased, feeling that the wished-for heir was born, and that I, whom he loved as a daughter, was through my trouble. He had a few friends to lunch with him, including my step-father, and said that he had seen all that he wished to see in life, and could now die happy at any moment. His guests left him in [the] greatest spirits, and two days afterwards he died, and his body had been brought back as I describe and he had been found half sitting and half lying in that very field-road, where I had three times seen him. He was dressed in the same homespun suit in which I had seen him in my dream. The cause of his death had been heart-disease, of whose existence neither I nor, I believe, any of those near or dear to him had been aware. He had evidently felt faint and slipped from his horse. The same two men whom I had seen in my dream as helping to carry the body had in fact done so, and my nurse admitted that the left hand knocked against the banisters. She seemed afraid lest I should blame the men who carried the body, and did not like to speak of the incident. I do not think that she had seen the incident herself; and I did not like to speak to the men about it. It was enough for me that it was on the back of the left hand, as I had seen it in my dream and as from the arrangement of the staircase it *must* have been, had it been caused in the way that I saw. (*Proceedings of the S.P.R.*, Vol. XI, 1895, pp. 577–9.)

Lady Q's step-father corroborated her account of what transpired when he met her in London to announce the news of her uncle's death, as did Lord Q, who was also present at this meeting.

It will be seen that, even in this case, not all the elements of the subject's dream corresponded directly and in a realistic manner to future events. The details of the flowers and snow were not correct, although Lady Q later discovered that dreams of flowers and snow were considered as symbolic of death by members of her family.

Not all cases of apparent precognition offer such a precise and complex correspondence with future events as this last case. A large number of other cases are clearly symbolic throughout.

The following is a case of an intermediate kind. It starts with an extract from a newspaper describing the incident apparently precognised.

YORK HERALD, *Friday, July 28, 1882*. 'SCARBRO'. SAD DEATH OF A GENTLEMAN VISITOR.—An accident of a melancholy character, and which unfortunately has been attended with fatal results, occurred on Wednesday evening to a London gentleman named Frederick Schweizer, who for the past few days has been staying at the Grand Hotel. It appears that on the afternoon of that day the deceased, along with a casual acquaintance named Deverell, who is staying at the Castle Hotel, went for a ride on horseback along the beautiful Forge Valley rides. When near Ayton the deceased was somewhat in advance of his companion, and it is surmised that his steed shied at a white gate; anyhow he was thrown on to the road, and the horse galloped away. His friend getting up to him dismounted, and a passing carriage was utilised to convey him to his hotel. This was at six o'clock, and three hours subsequently the deceased expired, it is supposed from concussion of the brain.'

The accident occurred on July 26th.

Mr. Schweizer's mother, Mrs. Schweizer, now of 6, Addison-road North, wrote on October 28th, 1882:—

I send you the particulars of the dream I had just eight days before it was realised, though why I could not be told of the unfortunate accident as it occurred I can't understand, nor why Henry Irving's name should be mentioned.—J. SCHWEIZER.

On the 18th of July I had the following dream or vision (I can't say which):- I was walking on the edge of a high cliff, the open sea in

front, dear Fred and a stranger a little in advance, when Fred slipped
suddenly down the side of the cliff, and in doing so gazed with the
most intense anguish into my very soul. I shall *never* forget that look.
I turned to the stranger and said, 'May I ask who you are and what is
your name?' He replied, 'My name is Henry Irvin.' I said, 'Do you
mean Irving the actor?' He said 'No, not exactly: but something after
that style.' I said, in reply, 'Now that I look at you, you have the same
agonised expression in your face that I have so often noticed in
Irving's photographs in the shop windows.' So I awoke in a miserable
state of mind. It was between 5 and 6 a.m. The servants came down
soon after. The dream seemed to haunt me; I could think of nothing
else. When I met my eldest son John, at breakfast, I asked at once,
where was Fred? (I must state here that Fred was the travelling
partner of three brothers, and then in the North of England on a
journey.) His brother, after hearing the dream, said, 'Oh, Fred is all
right; he is in Manchester.' He saw how miserable this dream made
me feel, and he promised at my request to 'wire' to me when he got
to his counting-house in case there was no letter from Fred, who was
in the habit of writing to the firm daily. There was, however, a letter
as usual, and when I received no telegram as arranged, I judged that
dear Fred was all right. Still the dream was present to my mind, and
I thought of it continually. I begged of his brother to tell him to come
home. In a day or two I heard he was at Leeds, and next day after
that, John the eldest brother said, 'Fred says he is going to take a
week's holiday at Scarborough,' when I at once exclaimed, 'I wish he
were at home; do write to him to come back; he has had holidays
enough this year. I shall write to him myself.' John said, 'Oh, don't;
let him enjoy himself.' On this day, before I got out of bed at the
same hour, between 5 and 6 a.m., a person seemed to pass the side of
my bed, and said into my ear in an audible voice, 'You are not done
with trouble yet.' I started up and awoke, and related the matter at
breakfast while talking of Fred to John, and said, 'I think it was your
father.' He said, 'Oh, nonsense, that is like the dream you bothered
me about a few days ago.' This was on the 23rd. On the 24th John
mentioned that he had a telegram from Fred to send on £10, that he
was enjoying himself immensely, that the weather was glorious. I
again wished he were at home, and John said, 'He will be here on
Friday next.' In the morning on the 26th I went to the letter-box, and
found a telegram for John, which announced an accident to Fred.
John, however, did not like to tell me, and hurried off to the office. I
asked John the nature of the telegram, but he said, 'Business.' On
arriving at his office, there was a telegram of a similar kind from the
hotel proprietor at Scarborough. Poor Fred was dead at the time, as
he only survived the accident three hours. John and I set off at once,
and found all over, and next day it was proposed that we should visit
the fatal spot. His companion in that unfortunate excursion accompanied us. He sat opposite to me in the carriage, and when I looked
at him I *remembered* the dream of the 18th, and recognised the stranger

who had the agonised expression, and asked him at once if his name were 'Henry.' He said, 'Yes, my name is Henry,' when I told the dream. He then said, 'The most extraordinary part is, I am connected with the Volunteers, and we have private theatricals, and I recite, and am always on those occasions introduced as Henry Irvin, jun.'

Mrs. Schweizer says that an account written by her, and substantially the same as the above, was signed by her son and by Mr. Deverell.

In answer to inquiries Mrs. Schweizer said (April, 1888): 'My son Frederick was not acquainted with Mr. Deverell at all, nor was Mr. Deverell known directly or indirectly to me or to any member of my family . . . We knew nothing about his private theatricals.' He was an acquaintance of a friend of Mr. F. Schweizer's and was only introduced to him by his friend on the afternoon of the accident, as a companion for the ride in which the friend could not join. (*Proceedings of the S.P.R.*, Vol. V, 1888, pp. 322–3.)

It is perhaps worth adding that the victim of the accident was away purely on business and he had already had a holiday shortly before, so, according to his mother, 'She was not in the least expecting him to have another, and had not the least idea, therefore, of his visiting the sea-side.'

In this case there are a considerable number of departures from complete realism. The mother only had a presentiment of a misfortune occurring to her son, and did not specifically foresee his death. Further, although the idea of misfortune was associated in her mind with the idea of her son falling, in the dream the son fell down a cliff, whereas in reality he fell from a horse. Finally, in her dream her son's companion revealed his association with the name of Henry Irving in a manner characteristic of dreams rather than of waking life, and which did not correspond exactly to the way in which he revealed it later in reality.

It appears most likely that we should regard all such perceptions as constructed by the subconscious mind to incorporate certain informational elements, but that in a very few cases the representation of a future event is so precise in every detail that it appears to the subject as if he was seeing in advance a future part of his experience. This is, of course, related to what we have said about the mimicry of normal perception which occurs in metachoric experiences.

We know that metachoric experiences may convey to the subject accurate information about his environment at the time, and may do so by presenting him with an imitative representation of his actual environment, which may be so exact that he takes it to be the world of normal experience, as in the typical spontaneous out-of-the-body experience. However, for various reasons we actually regard these representations of the normal environment as hallucinatory (see Chapter 12). In a similar way, the representations which are constructed to convey to the subject information about future events may, occasionally, correspond so precisely to the future event which he later experiences, that he regards it as a prevision of the actual experience.

*

Precognition is not a particularly favourable phenomenon to be given a primary position in a programme of research; at least, not at this stage in the development of our knowledge. I incline very much to the view that one's efforts should first be concentrated on those areas where definite and concrete information is crying out for someone to obtain it, such as lucid dreams and out-of-the-body experiences, and not on those phenomena where at this stage there is no obvious way of finding out anything about them.

Perhaps because precognition is felt to violate accepted beliefs about the nature of the world more than does extrasensory perception concerning approximately contemporary events, it is much less common for subjects to acquire techniques for producing precognition to order. Typically, it tends to occur in dreams—ordinary dreams, not lucid ones. Lucid dreams can be cultivated, so that phenomena which occur in them can be deliberately attempted by trained subjects. There is no known method of increasing the incidence of precognition in ordinary dreams, or making it more likely to occur on a given occasion.

The two cases we have already quoted in this chapter are both examples of apparent precognition occurring in non-lucid dreams. The following simple but striking case is a further example. The percipient was a Mrs. Atlay, wife of the Bishop of Hereford.

> My dream was as follows:-
> I dreamt that the Bishop being from home, we were unable to have family prayers as usual in the chapel, but that I read them in the large hall of the Palace, out of which, on one side, a door opens into the dining room. In my dream, prayers being ended, I left the hall, opened the dining room door, and there saw, to my horror, standing

between the table and the side-board, an enormous pig. The dream
was very vivid, and amused me much. The Bishop being from home,
when dressed I went down into the hall to read prayers. The servants
had not come in, so I told my governess and children, who were already there, about my dream, which amused them as much as it had
done me. The servants came in and I read prayers, after which the
party dispersed. I opened the dining room door, where, to my amazement, stood the pig in the very spot in which I had seen him in my
dream. With regard to your question as to whether I could have
heard the pig in my sleep, he was then safely in his sty, and my room
is quite on the other side of the house, a large hall dividing our side
from the servant's side of the house, behind which, in a yard, was the
pig-sty. It got into the dining room in consequence of the gardener
being engaged in cleaning out the sty while the servants were at
prayers; they having left every door open, the pig met with no
obstacle on his voyage of discovery.

FANNY P. ATLAY

I heard Mrs. Atlay tell the dream when she came into the hall
before prayers. [Precise date not remembered—a few years ago.]

EMILY NIMMO. (Governess.)
(Proceedings of the S.P.R., Vol. XI, 1895, pp. 487–8.)

Although some people claim to have precognition of some kind
in their non-lucid dreams fairly often, they have no control over
its occurrence. Consequently, it is virtually impossible at present
to see any direct method for studying the electrophysiological
characteristics of a subject's state at the time ostensible precognition is occurring. Even if we could do this, another difficulty
would arise from the fact that the kinds of precognition which
occur spontaneously are not very easy to assess. Dreams people
have which may refer to the future are often vague and symbolic,
and prolonged investigations and comparisons over a long period
of time would be necessary to determine which of their dreams
appeared to have a correspondence with future events that was
sufficiently unlikely on statistical grounds to be accepted as a
fairly definite instance of precognition. It would be quite possible
that other dreams, although genuinely precognitive, failed to come
up to the required standard, so that one would be restricted to the
study of a small number of dreams, which could only be selected
by the most laborious methods. Even when the laborious methods
had been applied, it would still be possible for critics to stigmatise
them as subjective, since however much attempt was made to
conduct the investigation with impartiality and mathematical

techniques, in the last resort the judgement whether a certain dream corresponds closely enough to future events to be regarded as definitely precognitive remains a subjective one.

A further difficulty is the fact that precognition is not something which people characteristically cultivate under conscious control. If it were found possible for lucid dreamers to attempt precognition with specific target material, this would be much easier to assess. For example, it would be possible to instruct lucid dreamers that they were deliberately to try to dream of, say, target symbols which would not be selected and set up by the experimenters until the next day. Provided they were experienced lucid dreamers, they should be able to remember this intention in their dream, and it would be possible to score their success in predicting the actual targets by the usual statistical methods.

A few subjects have in fact reported experiences of apparent precognition in lucid dreams, and it might be possible to cultivate it deliberately in them, but no one has yet tried.

The following example is reported by Dr. Frederick van Eeden:

> In May, 1903, I dreamed that I was in a little provincial Dutch town and at once encountered my brother-in-law, who had died some time before. I was absolutely sure that it was he, and I knew that he was dead. He told me that he had much intercourse with my 'controller', as he expressed it,—my guiding spirit. I was glad, and our conversation was very cordial, more intimate than ever in common life. He told me that a financial catastrophe was impending for me. Somebody was going to rob me of a sum of 10,000 guilders. I said that I understood him, though after waking up I was utterly puzzled by it and could make nothing of it. My brother-in-law said that my guiding spirit had told it to him. I told the story to somebody else in my dream. Then I asked my brother-in-law to tell me more of the after-life, and just as he was going to answer me I woke up,—as if somebody cut off the communication. I was not then as much used to prolonging my dreams as I am now.
>
> I wish to point out that this was the *only* prediction I ever received in a lucid dream in such an impressive way. And it came only too true, with this difference, that the sum I lost was twenty times greater. At the time of the dream there seemed not to be the slightest probability of such a catastrophe. I was not even in possession of the money I lost afterwards. Yet it was just the time when the first events took place—the railway strikes of 1903—that led up to my financial ruin. (*Proceedings of the S.P.R.*, Vol. 26, 1913, p. 451.)

Another disadvantage in investigating precognition is the diffi-

culty of excluding alternative explanations of ostensibly precognitive phenomena. The following case will serve to illustrate this
point. It was reported by a Mrs. Mackenzie.

July 14th, 1884

One morning last spring, when at breakfast, I suddenly remembered
a dream I had the night before, and told it to my house party, who
numbered 10 individuals. I should say that it was rather a joke against
me that I believed in dreams and that very often my dreams came
true; so when I mentioned having had a curious dream, I was greeted
with the usual joking remarks. 'Well,' said I, 'this is what I dreamt.
I thought there were several people in our drawing-room, among
others Mr. J., and I left the room for a few minutes to see if supper
was ready, and when I came back to the drawing-room I found the
carpet, which was a new one, all covered with black spots. I was very
angry, and when Mr. J. said it was ink stains, I retorted, "Don't say
so, I know it has been burnt, and I counted five patches." So ends the
dream.' Well we all went to church, it being Sunday, and on our
return Mr. J. came with us to luncheon, a thing he had never done
before, and some others joined our party. I went into the dining-
room to see if things were ready, and then going back into the drawing-room I noticed a spot near the door and asked who had been in
with dirty feet; being a new carpet I was particular. Mr. J., as in my
dream, said it was surely ink, and then pointed out some more spots,
when I called out, 'Oh! my dream! my new carpet! burnt!' As we
afterwards discovered, the housemaid had allowed the fire to go out,
and had carried in live coal from another room in a shovel, which she
had tilted against the door and spilt the coals on the carpet, burning
five holes. Of *course* next Sunday I had several offers from my party
to remain at home and watch the other carpets but I don't think that
housemaid will burn any more carpets.

J. W. MACKENZIE
(*Proceedings of the S.P.R.*, Vol. V, 1888, p. 343.)

This account was corroborated by Mrs. Mackenzie's daughter,
Miss Gertrude Mackenzie.

At first sight this seems a rather striking case of precognition
because of the very specific nature of the dream and the closeness
with which it corresponded to later events. However, on reflection
the following interpretation suggests itself, which only requires
one to postulate the operation of extrasensory perception. Once
Mrs. Mackenzie had had the dream her servant might have become aware of this fact by telepathy, and deliberately dropped the
coals on the carpet in order to make the dream come true. If it
seems unlikely that she would have jeopardised her job by doing
this consciously, one may suppose that the telepathy and the

decision to fulfil the dream took place subconsciously. We should also have to suppose that the other protagonist in the dream's fulfilment, Mr. J., found out about Mrs. Mackenzie's dream by telepathy, and when he saw part of it come true he decided, again subconsciously perhaps, to fulfil the part that concerned him. We might then liken this second part of the fulfillment to the way in which a person may sometimes see what is ostensibly the same apparition as that currently being perceived by someone else in his environment.

The same ambiguity of interpretation renders experimental investigation of precognition fundamentally unsatisfactory. We cannot rule out the possibility that, once the subject has declared his guesses on the selected targets which are to be determined at some future time, other people may become aware of his guesses by telepathy and unconsciously assist in bringing about the predicted result. For example, many methods of randomising involve the shaking and throwing of dice by human agency, and the person concerned may be able subconsciously to influence the fall of the dice in this process better than he is consciously able to. Even when no human agency is involved in selecting the targets, as when a mechanical dice-thrower is used, it is possible that psychokinetic influence could be exerted subconsciously by the subject himself, or by some other person, to bring about the predicted result. This difficulty cannot, at this stage of our knowledge, ever be eliminated from experimental work on precognition. Even when Professor J. B. Rhine went to the lengths of using weather conditions over the North Atlantic as a means of deriving his target sequence, the possibility still remained that someone's subconscious mind might have been prepared to go to the lengths of influencing the weather over the Atlantic to bring about the desired result. We may consider this improbable, but as we have so little knowledge of either precognition or psychokinesis it is difficult to see that such a subjective assessment of the 'probability' has any validity.

Incidentally, attempts to form judgements about the probability of various kinds of psychokinetic influence entering into experiments on precognition are only one example of a tendency people have to consider that, while practically nothing is known about the field of research in general, a good way of deciding on the correct interpretation of a given case is to form an opinion about what seems to them a probable or plausible way for these unknown faculties to go about things. Thus, for example, the then editor of the S.P.R.'s Proceedings, writing up the Chaffin Will case (see pp. 126-8), implies that it seemed to him most improbable that telepathic information concerning the whereabouts of the will, acquired before the old man's death, could have lain latent in the percipient's subconscious for so long a period of time (four years), and then emerged in a dramatised form.

I do not, of course, mean to rule out the possibility that if research in this field is one day enabled to commence on a meaningful scale, we may find one of our subjects, in the course of cultivating some other, more directly controllable state, producing precognition of a kind which would lend itself to investigation. If this were to happen, I should of course take advantage of it. However, it seems only reasonable to commence with those phenomena which lend themselves most directly and controllably to investigation.

The only type of research to which, at this stage, precognition obviously lends itself is the type of research which is aimed exclusively at adding to the evidence that it exists at all. Research of this kind, though I am only too painfully aware that many people see nothing at all wrong with it, has the draw-back that even if it succeeded in adding to the evidence for precognition in a striking manner, would do little to increase our knowledge of the process and the conditions under which it operates. It has the further draw-back that, like all research aimed at deriving an assessment of evidential value from spontaneous cases, it would be extremely expensive. It would first be necessary to obtain as many cases as possible, and then to investigate the ancillary circumstances of each case so as to derive some kind of an estimate of the unlikelihood of a coincidence between the alleged precognition and the corresponding event occurring by chance. However well work of this kind is done, it can still be called subjective by the scientific world, and is much more easily shrugged off than could be laboratory experiments in which every variable could be objectively measured.

Consequently, at the present time, I would not give precognition any but a very subordinate place in my research programme. This is not to say that I take a poor view of the prospects for studying it in the laboratory; it is only that this cannot be directly planned for. The various paranormal phenomena and the psychological states which favour them are inter-related, and it is very likely that when serious research is able to start on any of them, others may be found to occur spontaneously.

When discussing research in this field, people always talk as though no research can be done until every step of it can be exactly predicted in advance. This is to deny the essential nature of any research. (Even Sir Alexander Fleming found a penicillin mould growing on his culture-plate by accident and not design.) But it is particularly characteristic of paranormal processes that in studying one of them, you may easily find yourself confronted with another. However, finance is never available for this process to commence, and a serious programme of research worthy of the name with adequate laboratory facilities on any one phenomenon has yet to be undertaken. (It should be noted that Sir Alexander Fleming would not have discovered his penicillin if he had not had a culture-plate and a suitable laboratory to be studying it in.)

CHAPTER 16

Mediumship

IN the early days of psychical research, that is to say, during the short period before the volume of activity in the subject petered out on account of the decline of civilisation, a quite inordinate quantity of attention was devoted to the study of mediumship, and the reception of messages supposedly from deceased persons. The fact that so much energy was expended on this study was doubtless, in large measure, due to the fact that it was difficult to see how anything of a scientifically conclusive nature could result from it. The trance states of mediums appear to be somewhat idiosyncratic, and not to form a very definite class of states which could be studied physiologically in the way that lucid dreams and out-of-the-body experiences do. The evidence for the survival of human personality could never, in the nature of things, be conclusive. At best, the study of mediumship could produce convincing evidence for extrasensory perception of some kind, if the mediums were found to produce information which they could not have known by any normal means. This evidence was in fact forthcoming, but then it was forthcoming from many other sources as well; and mediumship viewed as a method for extending knowledge of extrasensory perception had little to recommend it.

However, many people professed to find the most burning interest in the question of whether human personality survived death, and immensely erudite investigations were undertaken by persons of the highest academic standing, in attempts to determine, for example, whether the range of classical allusions made in the voluminous productions of several automatic writers over a period of decades could be adequately accounted for by reference to the classical knowledge contained in the subconscious mind of one of the participants (several of whom were classicists) or whether it could only plausibly be accounted for by reference to continuing mental activity on the part of the deceased Myers. Personally, I have no inclination to attempt to assess 'plausibility' in contexts of this sort, although it seems to be one of the most spontaneous reactions of human psychology when it does make any attempt to think about the facts of psychical research. It is curious how ready people are to start asserting, say, that it seems to them 'most unlikely' that information telepathically acquired should lie latent in the subconscious mind for a given length of time before surfacing. When so little attempt has actually been made to study these functions of the mind as phenomena in their own right, but only to pile up evidence that they happen at all, I do not see what value can be attached to such assessment.

It should be pointed out that I am not accusing those who did take an interest in psychical research of any uncommon degree of silliness compared with the rest of academic mankind. This tendency to place great reliance on one's subjective feeling for what ought to be the case, and the preference for arriving at definite beliefs rather than merely considering the facts, is widespread to the point of universality. In fact, the most striking example possible of precisely these tendencies is provided by the modern academic world, which is so sure of its subjective feeling that paranormal phenomena ought not to exist, that it believes they do not.

However, the attempts of the psychical researchers to form a subjective assessment of the probability that human personality survived death were pursued with admirable thoroughness and pertinacity. They were fully aware of every possible way in which doubt could be cast on the value of evidence, and also of the usefulness of financial resources. They paid the best mediums they could find to work exclusively for them, and paid them well enough for them to agree to give sittings to no one else. They hired private detectives to observe their mediums, and to investigate all possible sources of information to which they might have access. Some of the results produced under these conditions are certainly striking as evidence for extrasensory perception.

One of the most remarkable cases studied by the early Society for Psychical Research was that of Mrs. Piper. She was an American, a married woman with two children, whose husband worked in a large store in Boston. She went into a form of trance-state, for which she was subsequently amnesic. In this state her normal personality disappeared and was replaced by someone who called himself Dr. Phinuit. Dr. Phinuit spoke in a man's voice, and in general his behaviour and manner of speaking were different from Mrs. Piper's normal personality. In this state Dr. Phinuit showed himself to possess information which Mrs. Piper apparently could not have known by normal means, and which he claimed to have received from other 'spirits' in the 'spirit-world'. Although he claimed to be a Frenchman, Dr. Phinuit did not appear able to speak in French; his performance as a doctor, however, was more tolerable, as he sometimes diagnosed illnesses correctly. This trance personality was generally referred to by the investigators as 'Dr. Phinuit', without, of course, this being held to assume more than that he was a part of Mrs. Piper's personality which was normally subconscious but which assumed control during the trance state. (The question of trance states and trance personalities is discussed at length in Myers' book *Human Personality*; it should be noted that the idea of a trance personality being part of the subject's subconscious personality was being used by Myers and the other investigators of Mrs. Piper some ten years and more before Freud published his views. The relationship between such dissociated states and ESP is discussed by Charles McCreery in his book *Science, Philosophy and ESP*, Chapter 9.)

Apparently this trance state first occurred to her spontaneously; later she found she was able to induce it semi-voluntarily, by 'a state of quiet expectancy or "self-suggestion"', as Myers puts it.

Mrs. Piper was first discovered by the famous psychologist William James, who reached the conclusion that there was no deception on the part of Mrs. Piper. He arranged with Myers for her to come to England for a period of two months in 1889-90, during which time she stayed either at Myers' house in Cambridge, or at Professor Lodge's house in Liverpool, or in a boarding house in London which was supervised by them. In the case which is given below one of the investigators, Sir Oliver Lodge, then Professor of Physics at Liverpool, describes how during this visit Dr. Phinuit gave certain details concerning the boyhood of an uncle of Lodge's. The verbatim record of the sittings Mrs. Piper gave during this visit (recorded by a stenographer) is given in the original reference, as well as an extensive discussion of the grounds for supposing that Dr. Phinuit showed evidence of ESP. We may remark here that the investigators both in America and England went to considerable trouble (and expense) in looking for evidence of deception on Mrs. Piper's part, including going to such lengths as hiring a detective to follow her as she did her shopping, and monitoring her correspondence. Mrs. Piper was apparently co-operative in all this.

It happens that an uncle of mine in London, now quite an old man, and one of a surviving three out of a very large family, had a twin brother who died some twenty or more years ago. I interested him generally in the subject, and wrote to ask him if he would lend me some relics of this brother. By morning post on a certain day I received a curious old gold watch, which this brother had worn and been fond of; and that same morning, no one in the house having seen it or knowing anything about it, I handed it to Mrs. Piper when in a state of trance.

I was told almost immediately that it had belonged to one of my uncles—one that had been mentioned before as having died from the effects of a fall—one that had been very fond of Uncle Robert, the name of the survivor—that the watch was now in possession of this same Uncle Robert, with whom he was anxious to communicate. After some difficulty and many wrong attempts Dr. Phinuit caught the name, Jerry, short for Jeremiah, and said emphatically, as if a third person was speaking, 'This is my watch, and Robert is my brother, and I am here. Uncle Jerry, my watch.' All this at the first sitting on the very morning the watch had arrived by post, no one but myself and a shorthand clerk who happened to have been introduced for the first time at this sitting by me, and whose antecedents are well known to me, being present.

Having thus ostensibly got into communication through some means or other with what purported to be a deceased relative, whom I had indeed known slightly in his later years of blindness, but of whose early life I knew nothing, I pointed out to him that to make Uncle Robert aware of his presence it would be well to recall trivial details of their boyhood, all of which I would faithfully report.

He quite caught the idea, and proceeded during several successive sittings ostensibly to instruct Dr. Phinuit to mention a number of little things such as would enable his brother to recognise him.

References to his blindness, illness and main facts of his life were comparatively useless from my point of view; but these details of boyhood, two-thirds of a century ago, were utterly and entirely out of my ken. My father was one of the younger members of the family, and only knew these brothers as men.

'Uncle Jerry' recalled episodes such as swimming the creek when they were boys together, and running some risk of getting drowned; killing a cat in Smith's field; the possession of a small rifle, and of a long peculiar skin, like a snake-skin, which he thought was now in the possession of Uncle Robert.

All these facts have been more or less completely verified. But the interesting thing is that his twin brother, from whom I got the watch, and with whom I was thus in a sort of communication, could not remember them all. He recollected something about swimming the creek, though he himself had merely looked on. He had a distinct recollection of having had the snake-skin, and of the box in which it was kept, though he does not know where it is now. But he altogether denied killing the cat, and could not recall Smith's field.

His memory, however, is decidedly failing him, and he was good enough to write to another brother, Frank, living in Cornwall, an old sea captain, and ask if he had any better remembrance of certain facts —of course not giving any inexplicable reasons for asking. The result of this inquiry was triumphantly to vindicate the existence of Smith's field as a place near their home, where they used to play, in Barking, Essex; and the killing of a cat by another brother was also recollected; while of the swimming of the creek, near a mill-race, full details were given, Frank and Jerry being the heroes of that foolhardy episode.

Some of the other facts given I have not yet been able to get verified. Perhaps there are as many unverified as verified. And some things appear, so far as I can make out, to be false. One little thing I could verify myself, and it is good, inasmuch as no one is likely to have had any recollection, even if they had any knowledge, of it. Phinuit told me to take the watch out of its case (it was the old-fashioned turnip variety) and examine it in a good light afterwards, and I should see some nicks near the handle which Jerry said he had cut into it with his knife.

Some faint nicks are there. I had never had the watch out of its case before; being, indeed, careful neither to finger it myself nor to let anyone else finger it. (*Proceedings of the S.P.R.*, Vol. VI, 1890, pp. 458–60.)

It is impossible for evidence produced by mediumship ever to produce conclusive evidence that human personality survives. When the medium produces information which he could not have known by any normal means, it is always possible that he has obtained it by extrasensory perception from the mind of some living person who knew about the facts in question, whether or not this person had anything to do with the séances. If the information produced was known to no living person (and it must clearly be very difficult to demonstrate this with certainty in any case in which there is any possible way of checking the information by reference to documents), two possibilities still remain. One of these is that the medium obtained the information by extrasensory perception of whatever document or source of information was used to check its accuracy, and the other that the medium obtained the information by retrocognitive telepathic perception of the information in the mind of the deceased person in question when he was alive.

The evidence provided by the degree of exactitude with which the medium is able to reproduce the mannerisms, tricks of speech, and habits of thought of the deceased person can also never be conclusive. The information on which such a dramatic reproduction is based could always be obtained by telepathy from the mind of the sitter, who is the person who is to be convinced. Or again, we cannot rule out the possibility that the medium might obtain the necessary information by retrospective telepathy.

As a matter of fact, behaviourists should, to be consistent, be the first to be convinced of survival by a realistic rendering of some deceased person's conversational mannerisms. In other contexts they will repeat indefatigably that what is meant by someone's individuality is the way he behaves, expresses himself and so forth.

One thing that did clearly emerge from the work of the Society for Psychical Research was the potentiality for dramatisation on the part of the subconscious, and another thing was the ability of the subconscious to remember things which had been consciously forgotten and to use them in later dramatisations. It is perhaps worth recalling these findings, since, as with other findings in this field, they were never generally known. In this particular case the result is that when new mediums, such as Rosemary Brown, appear, their productions are assessed without any awareness of preceding cases of a somewhat similar type.

CHAPTER 17

Conclusion, for the Particular Attention
of Millionaires

IT will I hope be clear that this book constitutes an appeal. I am still looking for the chance to do research, and able to offer superlatively good value to any millionaire who would like to finance something like me.

The desire to finance an exceptional person to do something exceptionally significant is not a very strong, or very frequent feature of human psychology.

Unfortunately I am not able to appeal to any other motivation, and my sole chance of achieving anything of any significance depends on my finding someone who is sufficiently exceptional in his own way to be able to wish me to be able to do something.

Now at present all I am able to do is to demonstrate dedication by staying put, restricting our activities within the available finances, which means selecting very small activities and carrying them out very slowly. Now I must admit that I find this awfully boring and think it is a fearful waste of my capacities.

I should be extremely grateful to be given an opportunity to get on with something. It has been the essential feature of my life that I have been prevented from using my abilities. My childhood was run by people who thought it undesirable that I should be allowed to take examinations, since that might make me appear different from other children; my adulthood has been surrounded by people who thought it quite undesirable that I should have any money to do research, since that might make me appear different from other adults. However, I have always been supposed to be a genius. Furthermore I am actually motivated to find things out. I have spent eighteen years since leaving college in establishing this

Institute in the hope that it might one day actually become large enough for something to be done in it. Even such a simple thing as establishing an Institute is quite difficult; I have done that and demonstrated the aforesaid dedication by staying put.

If anyone has the slightest interest in fundamental advances in knowledge, or in people with high I.Q.s having any chance to use them, would he kindly provide me with some money. Someone recently put up £10,000,000 to establish a new college. Considering how much there is to be done in this subject, that would be reasonable. £1,000,000 would still establish us on a qualitatively different basis from the present. £100,000 would enable us to expand somewhat, permanently. £10,000 would at least provide us with the wherewithal to get on with our present project for a year or so without being constantly checked in mid-stride by financial restriction.

Unfortunately I realise only too clearly that I am not the sort of person that most people are likely to wish to finance, but although I am sometimes tempted to disguise myself in the hope that I shall be supposed different from what I am, it has to be admitted that I cannot hope to compete with the genuine article in unoriginality.

Those who wish to support someone totally dedicated to the maintenance of belief in society will no doubt find many candidates for their money. Similarly, if they wish to find a safe and dull cause to finance, they will find many safer and duller than I can by any stretch of the imagination pretend to be. It must therefore be hoped that this book may reach someone who has the desire to finance someone like me, and the wherewithal to do it.

Aphorisms

The mature person never tells the truth when a lie will do.

*

The human race is so megalomaniac; they think you're being conceited if you say you're better than everybody else.

*

Human nature: vindictiveness lightly coated with dishonesty.

*

A human relationship is what happens when you know you can rely on the other person to be as dishonest as you are.

*

Psychotics frequently invert the truth about themselves. E.g.: 'It's love that makes the world go round.' (It's hatred that makes the world stay put.)

*

It is not so much that people don't want other people to have advantages; they want them not to have advantages.

*

The human race does not have much imagination, or (what comes to the same thing) much appreciation of reality.

*

It is impossible to be certain that any part of your experience is not a hallucination, or that any step in your thinking is not erroneous.

*

The human race believes in not taking its problems seriously enough to solve them.

*

If anyone says ethical values are supremely important, you may be sure he hasn't any.

*

People having religions is an insult to the universe.

*

The desire to maintain an uncritical belief in the reality of the external world is a source of emotional disturbance which leads to irrationality and restriction of function.

*

The female sex is a fictional concept.

*

On marriage: I can think of less painful ways of committing suicide.

*

If you think of women as human, they are exasperating on account of their incredible feebleness; of course, it's all right if you don't think of them as human at all.

*

People have been marrying and bringing up children for centuries now. Nothing has ever come of it.

*

A girls' school is a school for domestic servants.

*

Women are like sane people in general—you can't imagine how they can bear to be like it but the last thing they want is to be told how to stop.

*

The object of the educational system is to make the child feel suitably guilty for the harm that has been done to him.

*

Education by the State is a contradiction in terms. Intellectual development is only possible to those who have seen through society.

*

The word 'education' means 'leading out'. To execution, perhaps.

*

Women are the last people to be trusted with children. Those who have repressed their own aspirations will scarcely be tolerant of the aspirations of others.

*

If my education taught me one thing it was this: that if you are ever in a tight corner you can expect everybody to turn on you with all they've got. This is an infallible law of sane psychology.

*

There are some things that are sure to go wrong as soon as they stop going right.

*

The human race appears to cultivate feeble-mindedness. But this feeble-mindedness is not applied indiscriminately.

*

In the country of the blind the one-eyed man is lucky to escape with his life.

*

I decided to postulate infinitely many dimensions on grounds of economy of hypotheses.

*

A committee may be less likely than an individual to misuse funds; the question is whether it is equally likely to use them.

*

What is scandalous is not that stupid people should sometimes inherit private incomes; but that clever people should sometimes not.

*

The human race knows enough about thinking to prevent it.

*

Modern Definitions:
'Thinking *is* words, consciousness *is* behaviour, experiment *is* measurement.'

*

One of the greatest superstitions of our time is the belief that it has none.

*

Lack of clarity is always a sign of dishonesty.

*

A hundred trained people will never add up to one motivated one.

*

When you point out things which the human race has been carefully ignoring for centuries, on account of deep-seated emotional resistances, the expected outcome is not instant acclamation.

*

It is one of the major achievements of the human race that as its control of its environment increases, everyone becomes more— not less—immersed in the material.

*

That society exists to frustrate the individual may be seen from its attitude to work. It is only morally acceptable if you do not want to do it. If you do want to, it becomes a personal pleasure.

*

The most I ask of society is that it should express the will of the majority in a blind and imperfect manner. That would at least give one a sporting chance of survival.

*

Earning a living is regarded as moral. This is because a person who is answerable only to himself may or may not be wasting his time; an employed person is certain to be.

*

When the French Revolution decided to guillotine Lavoisier, he asked for a fortnight's grace to finish some experiments. The reply was that the Republic had no need of such things. The guillotining of Lavoisier was the true objective of the Revolution. It desired to destroy him so much that it was prepared incidentally to destroy any number of less intellectual persons *en route*.

*

We live in an age when humanity believes in itself. It believes in itself very thoroughly indeed. It is the beginning and the end to itself, its own solution to every problem. Humanity knows that philosophy was made by it, and religion was made by it, and society was made by it. In fact, reality was made by it. For (thus runs the reasoning) the agreement of a multiplicity of persons *is* the criterion we adopt for reality. There is no other criterion for determining reality. There is no other sense in which the word 'reality' can be used. Therefore reality *is* what a collection of people agree to call by this name.

*

Thus Newton: 'It is inconceivable that inanimate brute matter should, without the mediation of something else, which is not material, operate upon and affect other matter *without mutual contact*. . . . That gravity should be innate, inherent and essential to matter, so that one body may act on another, at a distance, through a vacuum, without the mediation of anything else, by and through which their action and force may be conveyed from one to another, is to me so great an absurdity, that I believe no man, who in philosophical matters has a competent faculty of thinking, can ever fall into it.' It is, if you give it a little thought, equally inconceivable that brute matter should operate upon and affect other matter *with* mutual contact. It does not seem so simply because, in the course of your life, you have become familiar with certain strange ways of affecting your environment called 'pulling' and 'pushing' things.

*

Adler once said that a genius is a person who contributes the most to the welfare of the human race. An unrecognised genius is impossible. So much for the compassion of Adler. There are no prisoners in the Bastille. Prisoners in the Bastille *do not exist*.

So much, also, for Adler's powers of analytical thought. Redefining a word does not annihilate its original meaning. You could define geniuses as people of high ability who wanted to use it (for example). If you say a crow is not a large black bird, but a small white animal that says baa, the species originally known as crows goes on living in the world with all their problems intact, even if these problems are quite different from those of woolly lambs.

*

Psychology used to deal with introspection. We have decided that introspective reports are unreliable. (So they are—sane people don't practise introspection hard enough to become accurate.) The conclusion was that we would abandon the study of introspection and study only 'behaviour'. It is easier to study the 'behaviour' of rats than people, because rats are smaller and have fewer outside commitments. So modern psychology is mostly about rats.

*

Adler suggested that the best guide to what a person was actually motivated to bring about was provided by a study of his life-style—i.e. a study of the situations that recurred in his life—rather than of what he said he was aiming at.

This principle might be applied to collective entities such as

organisations, societies, and the human race *in toto*. There is no
need to postulate a group subconscious in order to do this. The
combined subconscious motivation of the individual members is
quite sufficient to produce a resultant nexus of forces which will
permit certain developments and not others.

It is then clear that the history of the human race is to be understood as a prolonged effort not to gain control of its environment.

*

Tugging hard at its bootlaces, the human race resists with moral
indignation any suggestion that it might walk instead. 'Want us to
stay here for ever, don't you,' it says, puffing away.

Glossary

This glossary is in logical, not alphabetical, order, as some of the concepts depend on others which need to be explained previously.

A *lucid dream* is a dream in which the subject is aware that he is dreaming.

A *pre-lucid dream* is one in which the subject considers whether he is dreaming. He may or may not come to the correct conclusion that he is.

A *false awakening* is a dream in which the subject seems to wake up in bed, or elsewhere, in the normal way. It may then occur to him to doubt whether he is really awake, and he may proceed to examine his environment in the hope of obtaining clues. Sometimes he realises that what he is experiencing is only a dream in which case a lucid dream may follow.

The phenomenon of the false awakening may occur after both lucid and non-lucid dreams, but it seems to be particularly common among subjects who have frequent lucid dreams.

An *out-of-the-body* or *ecsomatic* experience is one in which the observer seems to himself to be observing the normal world from a point of view which is not coincident with that of his physical body.

A *metachoric* experience is one in which the subject's normal environment is completely replaced by a hallucinatory one. The most obvious examples of such experiences are dreams and lucid dreams. It should be noticed that although the subject's environment is temporarily completely hallucinatory it may provide an exact, or nearly exact, replica of his real one, as in a false awakening or an out-of-the-body experience.

In a *waking dream* the subject's environment is completely replaced by a hallucinatory one, as in an ordinary dream, except that the subject is awake and not asleep at the time.

Extrasensory Perception (ESP). 'A term of very general scope used to cover all cases in which knowledge of things or events is acquired by a person, in whatever manner, without the use of the ordinary channels of sense-perception, of logical inference or of memory.' G. N. M. TYRRELL, *Science and Psychical Phenomena.*

Telepathy. 'The communication of impressions of any kind from one mind to another, independently of the recognised channels of sense.' F. W. H. MYERS, *Human Personality.* (The term 'telepathy' was coined by Myers.)

Psychokinesis (PK). 'Used of alleged supernormal movements of objects, not due to any known force.' F. W. H. MYERS, *Human Personality.*

Precognition. 'A knowledge of impending events supernormally acquired.' F. W. H. MYERS, *Human Personality.*

Parapsychology. The scientific study of ESP, PK and related phenomena.

EEG (Electroencephalogram). A record of the electrical activity of the brain.

Alpha Rhythm. EEG waves of a frequency between 8 and 13 cycles a second.

Bibliography

SIR WILLIAM CROOKES, F.R.S., 'Notes of Séances with D. D. Home', *Proceedings of the Society for Psychical Research*, London, Vol. VI, 1889, pp. 98–127.

THE EARL OF DUNRAVEN, 'Experiences in Spiritualism with D. D. Home', *Proceedings of the Society for Psychical Research*, London, Vol. 35, 1924.

The Empiricists (An anthology of the writings of Locke, Berkeley and Hume), Dolphin Books, New York.

THE HON. EVERARD FIELDING, W. W. BAGGALLY and HEREWARD CARRINGTON, 'Report on a Series of Sittings with Eusapia Palladino', *Proceedings of the Society for Psychical Research*, London, Vol. 23, 1909, pp. 309–569, reprinted in *Sittings with Eusapia Palladino*, University Books Inc., New York, 1963.

OLIVER FOX, *Astral Projection*, University Books Inc., New York, 1962.

CELIA GREEN, *The Human Evasion*, Hamish Hamilton, London, 1969.

CELIA GREEN, *Lucid Dreams*, Hamish Hamilton, London, 1968.

CELIA GREEN, *Out-of-the-Body Experiences*, Hamish Hamilton, London, 1968.

CELIA GREEN and CHARLES MCCREERY, *Apparitions*, Hamish Hamilton, London, 1975.

THE MARQUIS D'HERVEY de SAINT-DENYS, *Les Rêves et les Moyens de les Diriger*, Cercle du Livre Précieux, Paris, 1964 (first published: Paris, 1867). An English translation of the Marquis's lucid dreams appears in *Psychical Phenomena and the Physical World* by Charles McCreery (q.v.), Chapter 7.

SIR OLIVER LODGE, F.R.S., 'Experience of Unusual Physical Phenomena Occurring in the Presence of an Entranced Person

(Eusapia Palladino)', *Journal of the Society for Psychical Research*, London, Vol. VI, 1894, pp. 306–60.

CHARLES MCCREERY, *Science, Philosophy and ESP*, Hamish Hamilton, London, 1972 (first published: 1967).

CHARLES MCCREERY, *Psychical Phenomena and the Physical World*, Hamish Hamilton, London, 1973.

F. W. H. MYERS, *Human Personality*, Longmans, Green & Co., London, 1903.

H. F. SALTMARSH, *Foreknowledge*, Bell, London, 1938.

G. N. M. TYRRELL, *Apparitions*, Gerald Duckworth, London, 1943.

G. N. M. TYRRELL, *The Personality of Man*, Penguin, London, 1947.

Index

THE HUMAN EVASION
Celia Green

The Human Evasion is an attack on the way of thought of twentieth-century man, revealing the patterns of prejudice which underlie his most cherished and sacrosanct opinions. For all its seriousness, the book is written with sustained wit and intellectual audacity. Surveying the whole field of modern thought, the author reveals the same disease at work in modern Christianity as in theoretical physics. Trenchant and provocative, this book is profoundly controversial—and brilliantly funny.

'Anyone who reads this book . . . must be prepared to be profoundly disturbed, upset and in fact *looking-glassed* himself; which will be greatly to his advantage, if he can stand it. Few books, long or short, are great ones; this book is short and among those few.'—*R. H. Ward*

'A subtle and sustained attack upon contemporary ways of thought.'—*Times Literary Supplement*

'Very witty.'—*The Guardian*

'Refreshing . . . so much sparkle.'—*Philip Toynbee, The Observer*

Hardback: £1·75   SBN 241 01756 5

HAMISH HAMILTON

LUCID DREAMS

Celia Green

Foreword by Professor H. H. Price, F.B.A., B.Sc.

Lucid dreams—dreams in which the subject knows that he is dreaming—raise important questions for philosophers and psychologists. If someone can reflect rationally while he is asleep, are we to say he is 'conscious' or 'unconscious'? If someone can critically examine his environment, asking himself whether he is dreaming, and conclude that he is not (although he is), what criterion can we use at any time to decide whether we are awake or asleep?

The first to recognise the scientific importance of lucid dreams, Celia Green has written what is likely to remain the classic study of the subject.

'A close study, unbiased and precise, of a fascinating subject, together with a wealth of equally fascinating examples.'— J. B. Priestley

'. . . the author should be congratulated on her choice and treatment of a subject on which so very little previous work has been done.'—*Times Literary Supplement*

'This fascinating book raises interesting questions which will doubtless form the basis of experimentation.'—Professor W. J. H. Sprott, *The Listener*

Hardback: £1·75   SBN 241 01758 0

HAMISH HAMILTON

OUT-OF-THE-BODY EXPERIENCES
Celia Green

Foreword by Professor H. H. Price, F.B.A., B.Sc.

If someone can perceive his surroundings in an apparently normal way, but from a position which is different from that of his physical body, this is a matter which our theories of sensory perception cannot afford to ignore.

We have also to consider whether someone who has emotional and intellectual experiences while his physical body is unresponsive to external stimuli should be said to be 'conscious' or 'unconscious'; how it is that someone can continue functioning in an apparently normal way while his 'consciousness' is concerned only in watching his movements from an external point; and what evidence for extrasensory perception is provided by the information obtained by the subjects of out-of-the-body experiences.

Celia Green's is the first extensive and systematic study of this field, based on a collection of 400 cases made by the Institute of Psychophysical Research, many of them quoted in full.

'It seems to me an admirable piece of work. I particularly liked the classification of cases, and I found the style refreshingly clear and readable.'—Professor Sir Cyril Burt.

'The present volume is the first in which contemporary instances are collected, collated and studied . . . the results are extraordinarily interesting, stimulating and well worth examining by the reader.'—*Times Literary Supplement*

'With this rich lode of material at her disposal Miss Green has been able to make an exciting advance in the clarification of her subject.'—*The Tablet*

Hardback: £1·75   SBN 241 01759 9

HAMISH HAMILTON

APPARITIONS

Celia Green and Charles McCreery

Mankind has been perennially fascinated by the subject of apparitions—or experiences in which ordinary people in everyday life have perceived things in their environment which were not really there.

The authors advance the highly original idea that when someone sees an apparition, not only is the figure of the apparition hallucinatory but the whole of the rest of the percipient's environment as well. This novel and at first surprising conception enables them to relate experiences of seeing apparitions to other unusual states of consciousness, notably lucid dreams and out-of-the-body experiences. It also enables them to explain for the first time certain hitherto puzzling features of apparitions, such as the fact that they are usually quite solid-looking and not transparent.

Their argument is illumined at every stage by the quotation in full of over 200 first-hand accounts, the majority taken from the Institute's own collection of over 2,000 cases. Among them are some truly remarkable experiences. There are cases in which people held long conversations with apparitions of the dead, and sometimes even touched or shook hands with them; apparitions that seemed to open locked doors, or walk or float in the air; apparitions of dogs, cats and even a rabbit; apparitions of houses and flowers.

The authors have produced for the first time a complete natural history of the hallucinations of the sane—their circumstances, subject-matter, duration, emotional accompaniment, illumination and so forth.

'This is a unique book, and has impressed me deeply.'—James Kirkup

'In my view no one who is interested in the subject should neglect this book.' The Rt. Hon. Lord Ogmore, P.C.

'An excellent piece of documentation, soberly treated, and well worth reading.'—Anthony Powell, *The Daily Telegraph*

'Enthralling.'—*Manchester Evening News*

'A fascinating and thought-provoking book.'—*Coventry Evening Telegraph*

Hardback: £3·75

SBN 241 89182 5

HAMISH HAMILTON

PSYCHICAL PHENOMENA AND THE PHYSICAL WORLD
Charles McCreery

Foreword by Sir George Joy, K.B.E., C.M.G.

A brilliant discussion, with numerous detailed examples, of extrasensory perception, psychokinesis, out-of-the-body experiences, apparitions, 'materialisations' and lucid dreams.

It also contains the first full account of the experiments carried out by the Institute of Psychophysical Research on birth order and extrasensory perception, in which it was found that eldest children tended to score better than others in a series of card-guessing tests.

Finally, Mr. McCreery discusses the experiments carried out in America which have confirmed the prediction made in his earlier book, *Science, Philosophy and ESP*, concerning the acceleration of the alpha rhythm in the ESP state.

> 'This excellent book cites numerous detailed examples and discusses the various philosophical questions involved. It should be of great interest to philosophers, to those concerned with the psychology of perception and, in my opinion, it has implications for the theory of art.'—Professor Colin Cherry

> 'Alarming clarity. . . . This absorbing book . . . succeeds in shaking up any comfortable assumptions about the nature of perception, the perceiver and the perceived in which the reader may previously have reposed.'—*Times Literary Supplement*

> 'Written with clarity and objectivity.'—*Nature*

> 'The real thing. . . . A fascinating and well-written book.'—*Kingston News*

Hardback: £2·30   SBN 241 02340 8

HAMISH HAMILTON

SCIENCE, PHILOSOPHY AND ESP
Charles McCreery

Foreword by Professor H. H. Price, F.B.A., B.Sc.

The phenomena of extrasensory perception and psychokinesis present a disturbing challenge to accepted ways of thought, suggesting that we may need to rethink our attitudes to such fundamental matters as the mind-body problem and the relationship between time and causation.

Charles McCreery's book provides a fascinating introduction to the subject for the general reader. It assumes no previous knowledge of the subject, and numerous examples of both telepathic and psychokinetic phenomena are presented vividly, and discussed in detail.

Mr. McCreery also discusses the EEG or 'brain waves' of the ESP subject, and the relationship of meditation, Yoga and such drugs as mescalin and LSD to the ESP state.

The book concludes with actual predictions which need to be put to experimental test. As Professor H. H. Price writes in his Foreword, 'All these predictions are capable of being empirically tested, and it is highly desirable that they should be.'

Readers of this book willl be interested to know that the prediction concerning the acceleration of the alpha rhythm in the ESP state has recently been confirmed by work done in America.

'Charles McCreery's is one of the most interesting studies of the psi-function to appear in recent years. . . . Mr. McCreery writes clearly and readably, and has produced a most fruitful, lively and promising mode of psychical research.'—*Times Literary Supplement*

'. . . A landmark in the history of psychical research. It is a theoretical advance of the utmost importance.'—Sir George Joy

Hardback: £2·25   SBN 241 02218 5

HAMISH HAMILTON